THE JEWS IN AMERICA

THE JEWS
IN AMERICA

Frances Butwin

Lerner Publications Company · Minneapolis

Front cover: In the 1980s, Jewish Americans protested Soviet government rules that prevented emigration by most Soviet Jews. The sign at the right bears slogans in English, Russian, and Hebrew.

Page 2: The board of directors of a Jewish loan society met in Minneapolis in 1923. Loan societies provided low-cost loans to help Jews start small businesses.

1991 REVISED EDITION

The Library of Congress cataloged the original printing of this title as follows:

Butwin, Frances.
   The Jews in America. Minneapolis, Lerner Publications Co. [1969]
   107 p. illus., facsims., map, ports. 24 cm. (The In America Series)
   Traces the history of the Jews in the United States and their role in the political, cultural, and industrial development of the country. Also discusses the causes and origins of anti-semitism.
   1. Jews in the United States — Juvenile literature. [1. Jews in the United States] I. Title
E184.J5B83   301.451'924'073   68-31501
                                                     MARC
                                                      AC

ISBN: 0-8225-0246-1 [Library]
ISBN: 0-8225-1044-8 [Paper]

Manufactured in the United States of America

8   9   10   11   12   13   14   15   16   17   00   99   98   97   96   95   94   93   92   91

CONTENTS

1
THE JEWS IN EARLY AMERICA

This page is from a Hebrew Bible produced in Toledo, Spain, in 1491–only one year before the Spanish royalty forced all Spanish Jews to either become Christians or leave Spain.

The Link with Columbus

Though the first group of Jews to settle in the American colonies arrived in 1654, the history of the Jews in America begins with the exploratory voyages of Christopher Columbus. Columbus had managed to get a commission from the Spanish monarchy at a time when non-Christians in Spain were suffering major setbacks. As Columbus wrote in his diary, "After the Spanish monarchs had banished all the Jews from their kingdoms and territories, in the same month they gave me the order to undertake with sufficient men my voyage of discovery to the Indies."

6

In January 1492, Granada—the last stronghold of the Moors (Muslims) in Spain—had fallen to the Christian forces of King Ferdinand and Queen Isabella. At the end of March, the king and queen ordered all the Jews who would not convert to Christianity to leave Spain within four months. Between 200,000 and 300,000 Jews who refused to convert to Christianity were expelled from Spain in 1492. Their wealth and property were confiscated by the Spanish monarchy. The final expulsion of the Jews from Spain occurred on August 2, 1492—only one day before Columbus set sail. This coincidence influenced the makeup of his seafaring crew.

Five Jews who had been converted to Christianity were among the 90 voyagers who set out with Columbus. These converts were officially called *conversos* or New Christians, but in popular speech they were known as *Marranos*. Two of the Marranos with Columbus (men named Bernal and Marco) were physicians, and a third, Luis de Torres, was an interpreter. Columbus sent the first reports of his discoveries to two of the queen's ministers who had pleaded his cause and helped him with their own money—Luis Santangel and Gabriel Sanchez, who were also Marranos.

Though many Marranos held high places at the Spanish court and were quite wealthy, their status was not secure. The very word *marrano* was a term of contempt. (It meant "pig" in Spanish.) Some Marranos who had been converted against their will still practiced Judaism—the Jewish religion —in secret. They were under constant suspicion of heresy and often underwent questioning and torture.

The Golden Age in Spain

Conditions for Jews of the Iberian Peninsula (the peninsula where Spain and Portugal are located) had not always been grim. For about 600 years— starting in the 8th century and lasting into the 14th—the Iberian Jews had enjoyed a Golden Age, a period of freedom, prosperity, and intellectual development.

It began with the conquest of southern Spain by the Moors in 711. The Moors were Arabic-speaking Muslims from North Africa who had developed a brilliant civilization noted for its literature, art, medical science, astronomy, and mathematics. Because the Moors were tolerant of the Jews, great numbers of Jews flocked to Córdoba and other Spanish cities. These cities became not only centers of trade but also marketplaces for the exchange of ideas.

The Jews in the cities of Moorish Spain established their own communities and academies of learning. These academies produced religious as well as secular scholars, philosophers, poets, doctors, and linguists. Jewish scholars translated books from Hebrew, Greek, and Arabic into Latin; later Christian scholars found these Latin texts useful. Moses Maimonides (1135-1204) was a doctor of medicine, an astronomer, a Biblical scholar, and a philosopher. His most famous book, *Guide of the Perplexed*, wove religion, philosophy, and the natural sciences into a guide to proper conduct.

In the 11th century, the northern provinces of Spain united under Christian rulers and began to drive the Moors out of the Iberian Peninsula. In the savage wars that followed, the Jews were caught in hostilities between two religions—Islam and Christianity—that were not their own. Some Jews (among them Maimonides and his family) went back to North Africa. Others went to northern Spain, where, at first, the Christian rulers welcomed them. Both Spain and Portugal were glad to utilize the skills of the Jews in commerce and the sciences. Prince Henry the Navigator of Portugal employed a cartographer, Judah Cresques, who became known as "the map Jew" or the "compass Jew." Other Jews and Marranos compiled astronomical tables and other navigational aids that proved very useful as European explorers ranged farther from their home shores.

But the Golden Age dimmed as the Catholic church grew in power and began to overshadow the state. Officials of the Dominican order, a Catholic organization, dominated Spanish

Moses Maimonides

Catholicism. In their eagerness to make Catholicism universal in Spain, the Dominicans threatened Jews and members of other religious minorities. It was under this pressure that many Jews became New Christians—a conversion that was often more formal than real.

Catholic authorities, however, did not consider it sufficient for Jews to be baptized into the Catholic church. The church set up a tribunal, or court, which brought to trial any New Christians who were not zealous enough in following their new faith. This tribunal was called the Inquisition or Holy Office, with a Grand Inquisitor at its head. The Spanish Inquisition gained a reputation for cruelty and unjust punishment. Innocent Spaniards would be tortured until they confessed to whatever the inquisitor had charged them with. Confessions in hand, the inquisitor would order the death penalty. Thousands of victims were burned at the stake. The Spanish Inquisition sought out not only the Marranos but also people of other religions and Christians suspected of heresy. The Inquisition followed its victims to the New World and lasted in one form or another until the late 1700s.

At the time of Columbus's voyages, the Grand Inquisitor was Tomás de Torquemada, Queen Isabella's confessor. It was he who influenced the king and queen to sign the order that, in the words of Columbus, "banished all the Jews from their kingdoms and territories."

The Sephardim and the Ashkenazim

The Jews who were driven from Spain and Portugal fanned out over central and northern Europe, joining Jewish settlements that already existed or forming new ones. The country that proved most hospitable was Holland— a haven for religious and political dissenters of all kinds, including the English Puritans. For one thing, Holland was fighting for its own independence from Spain and perhaps for that reason welcomed Spanish exiles. For another, the Jews had skills that were useful to Holland in its efforts to develop as a mercantile and colonial

power. A large and influential Jewish community formed in Amsterdam.

Wherever the Jews from the Iberian Peninsula went, they brought not only their religious heritage but also their Spanish or Portuguese language and culture. These Jews were called *Sephardim*, or Sephardic Jews—from the Hebrew name for Spain, *Sepharad*. They are distinguished from another branch of the Jewish people, the Ashkenazim, a word derived from the Hebrew name for Germany, *Ashkenaz*. These Jews had settled in Germany in the early Middle Ages and developed a German-Jewish culture and language. In time, the category of Ashkenazim came to include Polish, Russian, and other Jews from eastern Europe.

The Sephardim and Ashkenazim all had the same religion, but their rituals differed somewhat. Furthermore, the Sephardim considered themselves to be of an older and more sophisticated tradition than the Ashkenazim and tended to keep themselves aloof. Among the earliest Jewish immigrants to America, Sephardic Jews were the most numerous.

New Amsterdam

In September 1654, a French ship, the *Ste. Catherine*, tied up at a wharf in New Amsterdam (the capital of the Dutch colony of New Netherland) at the tip of Manhattan Island. Aboard the *Ste. Catherine* were 23 Jews—

men, women, and children—tired, bedraggled, and penniless.

They had come from Recife, a port in northeastern Brazil where a large community of Sephardic Jews had lived under Dutch rule since the 1630s. They built a synagogue and had a community of 5,000. In 1654, however, the Portuguese—who were conducting their own Inquisition and who were not tolerant of Jews—gained control of Recife. Most of Recife's Jews sought refuge elsewhere. Many returned to Holland; some went to Suriname (Dutch Guiana) and others to Curaçao, Jamaica, Barbados, and other islands of the Caribbean. The group aboard the *Ste. Catherine* had originally headed for the Caribbean islands, but Spanish authorities there refused to allow the Jews to disembark. With few ports open

to them, they headed north to the Dutch settlement at New Amsterdam.

Peter Stuyvesant, the governor of Holland's New Netherland colony, did not want to harbor the Jews either, and he wrote letters back to his employers, the Dutch West India Company, complaining about the burden that these new arrivals would put on the colony. The company—which had several Jews on its board of directors and did not share Stuyvesant's biases—ruled that the Jews could stay. Stuyvesant, known for his strict loyalty to the Dutch Reformed church, was also reluctant to allow religious diversity in New Netherland. If he let the Jews in, he complained, he would soon have to allow Lutherans, Catholics, and other non-Calvinists into his domain. The Dutch West India Company, however,

Synagogue of the Portuguese Jews in Amsterdam, dedicated in 1674

saw no harm in letting the Jews worship in New Amsterdam.

Stuyvesant obeyed, but only grudgingly. The Jews were allowed to trade with the American Indians who lived near the Hudson and Delaware rivers, but not to enter the retail trade in the towns. New Amsterdam's Jews were not granted all the rights enjoyed by other residents of the colony, and they had to fight to get the few rights they did have. For example, the Jews were made to pay a tax (which most of them could not afford) instead of being allowed to serve in the militia. This policy was protested by one of the Jewish leaders, Asser Levy, who was eventually allowed to serve in the militia. The Jews even had difficulty getting permission to buy a plot of land for a cemetery.

In 1664, King Charles II of England sent his fleet to capture New Amsterdam and claim the land for England. He renamed the city New York, in honor of his brother, the Duke of York. Although many of the Jews who had lived in the Dutch colony eventually moved to other places, a community of Jews remained in what was now the British colony of New York.

New England

Jews came to the American colonies for the same reasons other colonists came—for political and religious freedom and for economic opportunity. Political rights, such as the right to vote, to hold office, and to serve in the militia, were granted to Jews in only a few places in the colonies. Jews were considered "an alien nation," even though they were not a nation at all. They came from many nations and spoke a number of languages, but they had their religion in common. Even in the colonies where the Jews did not have full civil rights, the practice of their religion was generally not denied to them.

In New England, especially—where the Puritans studied the Old Testament and gave their children such Biblical names as Nathaniel, Ezra, Ezekiel, Abigail, and Rachel—the Jews were looked upon with respect. The Puritans, however, believed that all the Jews would have to be converted to Christianity before Christ could return to earth and a new age of peace and plenty could dawn. The Puritans did not try to force this conversion, but they awaited it with hope.

A few conversions took place, often because Jews found a change of religion to be beneficial to their careers. The American colonies, like England, at first excluded Jews from colleges. (England did not grant degrees to Jews until 1871.) The first Jew to get a degree from Harvard College in Cambridge, Massachusetts, was Judah Monis, who had come from Italy. He received an M.A. degree from Harvard in 1720, but it appears that before he could get a teaching post he had to become a

Christian. In March 1722, Judah Monis was baptized at College Hall, Cambridge, and was appointed instructor in Hebrew. He taught Hebrew at Harvard until 1760 and published *A Grammar of the Hebrew Tongue*, the first Hebrew grammar to be published in America. Though he belonged to the First Church at Cambridge and left a bequest in his will to the widows of poor Christian clergymen, Judah Monis stuck to one tenet of his old faith. He always observed Saturday, not Sunday, as his Sabbath.

A more liberal attitude was taken in 1789 by the founders of Rhode Island College at Providence (later Brown University). The trustees provided for complete freedom of religion for all students and exempted Jewish students from attending Christian services. The college received gifts of money from Jewish merchants as far away as Charleston, South Carolina. A donation of lumber came from a rich merchant named Aaron Lopez of Newport, Rhode Island—where the second Jewish settlement in the North American colonies had been established in 1658.

The colony of Rhode Island had been founded in 1636 by Roger Williams, a young minister who believed in freedom of religion. That was one reason why the Jews came to Newport. Another reason was that Newport was a prominent seaport and commercial center. The Sephardic Jews who settled there had business connections in London and Amsterdam and soon built up trade with other American seaports. Early maps of Newport show Bellevue Avenue lined with shops owned by Jewish merchants of Spanish and Portuguese descent. The shipowners and traders had such names as Rivera, Lopez, Mendez, and Seixas.

The most prominent among them was Aaron Lopez, who came from Lisbon in 1752 and became one of the leading merchants of his day. He and his brother Moses owned ships that carried goods to Europe and up and down the Atlantic coast. Letters from merchants in South Carolina mention the exchange of such goods as rice, potatoes, nuts, rum, molasses, and casks of red and white Lisbon wine. Jacob Rivera, in association with others, began to process spermaceti (a waxy oil from whales), which was used in making candles and oil for lamps. By 1776, Newport's population of 7,500 included 1,200 Jews—the largest Jewish community in America at that time.

Before they built a synagogue and appointed a rabbi, the Jews of Newport used to write to friends and relatives in Amsterdam and London for advice about religious aspects of births, marriages, deaths, and the observance of holidays. It took a response so long to cross the ocean that they had to improvise their own rules. In 1763, the Jews of Newport built a synagogue designed in the Georgian style by Peter Harrison, an English architect. The

The Touro Synagogue in Newport, Rhode Island, was built on Touro Street in 1763.

Sephardic ritual was observed in this synagogue, which was named the Touro Synagogue in honor of its first officiating rabbi, Isaac Touro. It is the oldest synagogue in America still standing, and together with the Tuoro cemetery it has become a historic landmark of colonial America.

Pennsylvania

The first Jews in Pennsylvania came from New Amsterdam to trade with the American Indians along the Delaware River as early as 1655. Other Pennsylvanians considered these "Israelites," as they were called, a curiosity. In fact, some colonists believed that the American Indians were descended from the 10 lost tribes of Israel. William Penn, the founder of Pennsylvania, granted religious freedom—but not full civil rights—to the Jews who came to settle in his colony.

Early in the 18th century, Lancaster, Pennsylvania, which was an important frontier post for the western fur trade, had a small Jewish community that maintained a place of worship and a cemetery. In 1747, the Jews of Philadelphia held religious services in a rented room in Sterling Alley. Around that time, an advertisement in Benjamin Franklin's *Pennsylvania Gazette* asked that local hunters not use the brick wall at the Jewish cemetery as a target for shooting practice. It further stated that anyone who reported these "sportsmen" would receive a reward of 20 shillings from the person who had placed the ad, Nathan Levy. This Nathan Levy, who had bought the burial plot, was a well-to-do merchant, a prominent citizen, and a musician who "played a very good violine" at a concert in the Music Hall of Philadelphia.

Not all the Jewish settlers in Pennsylvania owned burial plots or belonged to musical societies. Most of them were pack peddlers who went into the wilderness to barter with the American Indians. In a typical trade, a Jewish peddler might exchange a brass kettle, a gun, or a bottle of rum for a bundle of deerskins. Other Jews on the frontier made a living by selling provisions to soldiers who were fighting the French and the American Indians.

Modern historians, however, can most easily learn about the lives of the colonists who left written records—business letters, newspaper notices, wills, and other documents. Businesspersons in the cities, not frontier traders, transacted business by letter, advertised in the newspapers, and drew up legal papers to leave money and silver plate to their heirs.

One of the families who left such records was the Gratz family. Barnard Gratz was born in a town in Upper Silesia on the Polish-Prussian border in 1738 and left home as a young boy to seek his fortune in London. He arrived in Philadelphia in 1754. At first he worked as a clerk for another Philadelphia merchant, David Franks. When Gratz heard that his brother Michael was planning to come to America, he wrote to him to bring from London about 20 silver watches, some "new-fashioned watch chains," 20 dozen women's shoes, and "a few dozen women's mittens in black worsted."

Within a few years the Gratz brothers were shipping to England cargoes of raw furs, cattle, grain, and lumber, presumably in exchange for more silver watches and women's worsted mittens. This was the pattern of colonial trade —raw materials from America in exchange for manufactured goods from Europe. Soon, however, England imposed heavy duties on the export trade. In protest against the Stamp Act, which taxed all legal documents, the colonial merchants banded together to sign a nonimportation agreement in Philadelphia in 1765, pledging themselves not to import goods from England until the Stamp Act was repealed. Among the signers of this agreement were Barnard and Michael Gratz.

The Jews of Philadelphia did not draw up plans for a synagogue building until the 1770s. The synagogue was built on Cherry Alley and dedicated in 1782, during the Revolutionary War. Its first rabbi was Gershom Mendez Seixas, who had been the rabbi of the New York congregation but who left during the British military occupation of New York City. This Cherry Alley synagogue was used as a house of worship by Philadelphia Jews until 1825.

South Carolina

The first Jew mentioned in South Carolina history, an interpreter, remains anonymous. When Governor John Archdale published *A New Description of that Fertile and Pleasant Province of Carolina* (London, 1707) he wrote of a remarkable incident that happened in 1695. Some American Indians "going a Hunting, about 200 miles to the Southward," had captured four Indians of a different tribe near St. Augustine, Florida, and brought them to Charleston (then known as Charles Town), intending to sell them as slaves. After interviewing the captives, the governor set them free. The Florida Indians, wrote the governor, "could speak *Spanish* and I had a *Jew* for an interpreter." This Jew may have been a former Marrano.

Charleston was a busy seaport and the largest and most cosmopolitan city in the South. It drew many Jews of Spanish descent who came from England and from the British possessions in the West Indies. Such names as Simon Vallentine, Jacob Mendis, and

The cemetery of Beth Elohim, the first Jewish congregation in Charleston, South Carolina. Some graves in the cemetery date from 1762.

15

Abraham Avilah are mentioned in early documents. They are described as "merchants," a term that applied not only to those in the shipping trade but also to peddlers and shopkeepers. South Carolina had a liberal constitution that, in its original draft, promised freedom of worship to "Jews, Heathens," and others. The final draft didn't mention the Jews specifically, but they enjoyed most of the privileges granted to other religious dissenters.

The first Jewish congregation in Charleston was organized about 1749. It was called *Beth Elohim* (meaning "the House of God"), and its services were conducted in the Sephardic ritual. It moved from place to place until 1794, when a synagogue was built. The building caught fire, however, in 1831. The Beth Elohim synagogue built 1840 to replace the burned-out structure is one of the oldest Reform synagogues in America. It stands on a plot of land donated to the congregation by the heirs of Joseph Tobias, who served as the president of the first congregation.

The *hazzan* (cantor) of that earliest congregation was Isaac Da Costa, a merchant who had come from London in about 1740. He did business with Aaron and Moses Lopez of Newport, Rhode Island, and carried on an extensive correspondence with them. In Newport, Isaac Da Costa met a Congregationalist minister, Ezra Stiles, who made a point of meeting well-educated Jews and discussing the Scriptures with them.

Another New England clergyman, Hezekiah Smith, came to Charleston in 1769 to raise funds for Rhode Island College. He found an enthusiastic supporter in Moses Lindo, who had studied at the Merchant Tailor's School in London but who, as a Jew, had not been officially registered or granted a diploma. Moses Lindo was a technologist specializing in the processing of dye from the indigo plant, which was grown in South Carolina and was, next to rice, the colony's largest item of export. Lindo had arrived in Charleston in 1756 to select, appraise, and ship indigo for a group of London textile manufacturers who used great quantities of the royal blue dye. Lindo also experimented with other vegetable dyes, including a crimson dye that he extracted from a South Carolina berry. Moses Lindo died in 1764, shortly before the Revolution put an end to trade with Great Britain and ruined South Carolina's indigo industry.

The Jews in the American Revolution

At the time of the American Revolution, about 2,500 Jews lived in the American colonies. (Some sources put their number as high as 3,000, others as low as 1,500.) In the total population of the 13 colonies (about 2.5 million), the Jews were a tiny but significant minority.

Like other groups of colonists, the Jewish communities in America included both Tories (persons loyal to the British crown) and Patriots (supporters of the Revolution). The Patriots, however, were far more numerous among the Jews in America. Jews took part in the revolutionary struggle from the start. Jewish merchants, in particular, vigorously opposed such British proclamations as the Navigation Acts and the Stamp Act, both of which placed burdens on commerce in the colonies. When fighting broke out, American Jews continued to support the Patriot cause.

Early in the war, many of the Jews of Newport chose to abandon their homes and businesses rather than collaborate with the British. Philadelphia —the gathering place for American Patriots—attracted Jews from Newport, New York, Charleston, and Savannah, Georgia. Non-Jewish Americans even saw in the Revolution a parallel to the ancient struggles of the Israelites. The Liberty Bell, which was cast 25 years before the Revolution, bears an inscription from Leviticus, a book of the Old Testament: "Proclaim liberty throughout all the land unto all the Inhabitants Thereof (Lev. XXV:10)."

Benjamin Nones, a Jew born in Bordeaux, France, came to Philadelphia in 1777 and joined in the colonial struggle against the British. Nones, who fought in all the battles of the Carolinas and at the siege of Savannah, became a colonel commanding 400 soldiers, many of whom were Jews. At the battle of Camden, South Carolina, Nones reportedly helped carry the critically wounded General Johann de Kalb—a German fighting on the Patriot side—from the field of battle. After the war, Benjamin Nones went to Philadelphia, where he became an official interpreter of French and Spanish for the new government.

Francis Salvador, who came from London to northwestern South Carolina in 1773, owned an indigo plantation. Elected to the South Carolina Provincial Congress (the colonial legislature), he was the first Jew elected to a popular assembly in North America. When the British fleet attacked Charleston, he joined the state militia and became an officer. Salvador's regiment defended South Carolina's back country against attacks by Tories and Britain's American Indian allies. On August 1, 1776, when his regiment was ambushed by American Indian forces, Salvador was shot down from his horse and then scalped. A plaque in Charleston dedicated to his memory reads:

Born an aristocrat, he became a
  democrat,
An Englishman, he cast his lot with
  America;
True to his ancient faith, he gave his life
For new hopes of human liberty and
  understanding.

Mordecai Sheftall, a native of Savannah, Georgia, was a prosperous

A statue in Chicago's Heald Square, commemorates three leading Patriots of the American Revolution. George Washington stands in the center, with Robert Morris (left) and Haym Salomon (right).

merchant and, according to the British, "a very great rebel." He was in charge of purchasing food and supplies for the fighting forces. Sheftall was so meticulous in his duties that he left numerous letters, accounts, and receipts behind—a good resource for research into day-to-day events of the war in the South. When Savannah fell, he was captured by the British, put on a prison ship with his son, and taken to the West Indies. During interrogations by the British, he suffered many humiliations both as a Jew and as a rebel. After the war, he received a grant of land from the American government in recognition of his services.

A monument in Chicago (erected in 1941) features three figures—George Washington in the center, Robert Morris on one side, and Haym Salomon on the other. Robert Morris was in charge of raising money to pay, feed, and clothe the Patriot army during the Revolution—a formidable task since Congress had no power to impose taxes. Loans came from France and Spain, but these were in the form of notes that had to be cashed or "discounted." Haym Salomon was the broker who discounted these notes. More than that, he made personal loans to Thomas Jefferson, James Madison, and other delegates to the Continental Congress. James Madison, who was to become the fourth president of the United States, wrote to his friend Edmund Randolph that he was resorting to loans from Salomon, "with great mortification," because Salomon "obstinately rejects all recompense.... To a necessitous delegate he gratuitously spares a supply out of his private stock."

Haym Salomon, this generous financier, was born in Lissa (Leszno), Poland. Having left home as a boy, Salomon traveled all over Europe, learned many languages, and acquired a thorough knowledge of banking and finance. In 1772, after Poland was divided up by more powerful European nations, he went to London. Two years later he came to New York and began building friendships with American patriots. Salomon was arrested by the British as a spy and condemned to death, but somehow he escaped and went to Philadelphia, where he met and began assisting Robert Morris. Salomon also donated a large sum of money to the building of the Philadelphia synagogue in 1782, and later he sent money through Amsterdam business agents to his needy parents in Poland. Though he had handled large sums for the American government, his personal assets at the time of his death were quite small.

When the Revolution ended, each of the 13 new states had its own constitution and its own set of laws. Some had religious restrictions on voting and holding office, rules that effectively kept Jews out of public office. Thomas Jefferson, then governor of Virginia, opposed such restrictions. In 1786, Virginia passed the Statute of Religious Liberty, which gave equal civil rights to people of all religions. Soon the other states followed Virginia's example.

A map by Judah Cresques, a Jewish-Portuguese cartographer

2
THE JEWS FROM GERMANY AND CENTRAL EUROPE

Like many Jewish immigrants to America, this man "cashed clothes"–bought and sold used clothing–for a living.

Medieval Myth

Until well into the 19th century, few Christians in Europe mingled with Jews on an equal footing. Jewish communities were common in medieval Europe –in Spain, Italy, France, the Rhineland, Bohemia, and many other regions –but the Jews were excluded from Europe's feudal society. Jews could not own land or work on it. They were considered the king's property, and he could do with them as he pleased. If he found them useful, they stayed; if not, he expelled them. Some Jews found places as a king's personal physicians, or as moneylenders and treasurers who provided the money the European monarchs needed to fight their wars. In return, a king might give protection to a favored Jew, but medieval monarchs and nobles generally gave about as much respect to their "court Jews" as they did to court jesters or troubadours.

Jewish craftspersons (such as goldsmiths, weavers, tailors, or shoemakers) were not admitted to the guilds organized by skilled workers, because these guilds were for Christians only. Jewish merchants had to pay heavy taxes for the privilege of doing business. In many locations, they had to pay taxes simply for permission to live in the town. They were not given full civil rights, could not hold office, and could not mingle freely with the other townspeople. But as long as they could work, they managed to get along and sometimes to prosper.

On the European continent and in England, the feudal vassals, who were tied to the land and oppressed by the nobles, looked upon the Jews with hatred and suspicion. The Jews seemed to have more freedom than they. In contrast to the great majority of Europe's people, many Jews were educated and literate—they knew how to read and write and often spoke more than one language. Above all, they knew the language of numbers. They could do sums and handle coins with ease. Besides, the Jews practiced a different religion from their neighbors, followed strange customs, observed their own holidays, and ate different foods. Weird, absurd tales were told about these mysterious people: they were devils in disguise; they had tails like monkeys, hidden under their long cloaks; they used Christian children's blood in their rites; they practiced witchcraft. The clergy and nobles found it to their advantage to encourage these tales. If a peasant lost his bit of land, if the crop failed, or if a child died of the plague, someone had to be blamed. It was easy to lay the blame on the Jews.

The Roman Catholic church, a powerful social force in medieval Europe, held that it was wrong to charge interest on loans. Since very few people were willing to lend money without charging for the service, the entire moneylending business was opposed by the church and had a bad reputation among the general populace. This despised calling was shifted onto the Jews, even though Judaism also forbade usury—the charging of excessive interest on loans. The law permitted moneylenders to accept "pledges" from the borrowers, but, when the borrowers could not pay back their loans and the Jewish moneylenders collected on these pledges, the Jews were accused of greed. Although their profits were precarious—kings and nobles sometimes simply seized the assets of Jews—moneylenders accumulated some wealth in the form of armor, jewels, houses, and precious metals.

Consequently, a stereotype of Jews arose, a nasty image of the diabolical, miserly Jew who owned treasures that everyone coveted. William Shakespeare drew on this image when he created the characters of Jessica and her miserly father, Shylock, in *The Merchant of Venice*. By Shakespeare's time (1564-1616), this unflattering reputation had been troubling Jews for several hundred years. Shakespeare, however, was unlikely to have known many Jews himself. Although Jews had come from France with William the Conqueror in 1066, England's Jews were expelled in 1290 and were not allowed to return until Oliver Cromwell gave them permission to do so in 1656.

The Ghetto

Nearly every city in Europe had its Jewish quarter—a neighborhood where most of the city's Jews lived. In imperial Rome, this neighborhood was called by a Latin name—*Vicus Judaeorum*. In Spain it became *Judaria*, in France *Juiverie*, in Germany *Judengasse*, in Austria and Bohemia *Judenstadt*. Often these quarters grew up naturally near a Hebrew academy, a busy marketplace, or a synagogue. Living close together, the Jews felt safer from outside attack.

In the 16th century, these Jewish quarters became known as ghettos. No one is sure about the origin of the word *ghetto*, but the most commonly held theory is that it came from the word *giotto*, a cannon foundry near which the Jewish quarter in Venice was located. It was at about this time that the ghettos became places where the Jews were forced to live, not where they chose to live.

In 1556, Pope Paul IV established the first compulsory ghetto in Rome on the left bank of the Tiber. The Roman ghetto was enclosed by a high wall and had a gate that was locked from sundown to sunrise, as well as on Sundays and Christian holidays. The Jews were not allowed to live anywhere else in the city. It became a model for such ghettos in the rest of Europe.

The restrictions on Jews varied from place to place. In nearly every European city, the Jews were made to wear a yellow badge, a peaked hat, a long gaberdine (a loose smock), or some other distinctive garment. In Rome, they had to march in a procession once a year carrying their *Torahs* (scrolls on which the first five books of the Scriptures were written) and beg permission of the Pope to allow them to remain another year. In most places they paid a heavy tax. If they were allowed to trade outside the ghetto walls, this trade was limited by various rules. For instance, they might sell used clothing (but not new garments), old jewelry, and secondhand goods of all kinds. The Jewish merchants, restricted to an inventory of old clothes and junk, could not help looking shabby. Going through the marketplace with their yellow badges, carrying their stock of used goods in and out of the ghetto, they were often jeered and insulted by other people.

The ghettos soon became overcrowded. New storeys had to be added on top of old houses. The streets were narrow, gloomy, and often dirty. Little sunlight and air penetrated the densely built-up areas. When the compulsory ghettos were finally abolished, the term *ghetto* continued to be applied to any poor and crowded neighborhood occupied by Jews or other minority groups.

Life in the European ghettos, however, was not always mean and squalid. In Frankfurt, Trieste, and Prague, the ghettos were cities within cities. Mayer Amschel Rothschild (1743-1812), the founder of the Rothschild banking family, had an impressive house in the Frankfurt ghetto. The Prague ghetto was famous for its Talmudic academies, to which Hebrew scholars flocked from all over Europe. The Jews of Prague had an autonomous government, with a chief rabbi, a council of elders, and their own courts of law. They had their own town hall and four craft guilds—for goldsmiths, tailors, butchers, and shoemakers. Holidays were celebrated with pageantry, feasts, and processions. Once a year, in a festival called *Purimspiel*, troupes of players put on masks and costumes and enacted a play about the scriptural story of Queen Esther and Haman. At times, the religious leaders in the ghetto exhorted their people to pay less attention to feasting and fine clothing—and more to prayers and acts of piety. Such warnings echoed the exhortations so often made by the prophets of old to the people of Palestine.

Even while the ghettos were becoming a way of life for the Jews of western Europe, threats to Jewish security grew. Crusaders who gathered to march against the Muslims in the Holy Land first turned against the non-Christians at home. With a cry of "Death to the Christ-killers!" fanatical mobs roamed the cities, looted and burned Jewish homes and synagogues, and tortured and killed those who tried to defend themselves. Some Jews, rather than give up their faith or submit to torture, chose to commit suicide. In a few cases, mothers killed their children and then leaped into the Rhine and drowned. Many young men died trying to repel attacks on their neighborhoods. Elderly men marched in processions carrying their sacred scrolls and chanted *"Shema Isroel"* ("Hear, oh Israel") as they were being beaten to death by Christian marauders.

Another threat to the Jewish communities was the Black Death, or bubonic plague, that ravaged Europe in the 12th and 13th centuries. In their ignorance of what caused the plague, people blamed the Jews for it. The Jews were accused of casting evil spells and poisoning the wells and rivers. Many residents of European cities believed that if the Jews were driven out, the plague would go. Jews from many parts of western and central Europe actually were expelled from their homes and had to look about for new places of refuge.

Poland

On the wide, fertile plain east of Germany lived a Slavic people who, having been converted to Roman Catholicism in the 10th century, fought off several invasions by Tartars from the east and formed the kingdom of Poland. Poland was an agricultural country made up of large estates owned by nobles, or *pans*, and cultivated by peasants. A middle class was needed to build up the towns and develop trade with the other nations. For this purpose, the Polish kings began to import German traders and craftspersons, and in 1264, King Boleslav invited the Jews from Germany to settle in Poland. As an inducement, he issued a charter that gave the Jews freedom to travel and offered them protection from attack. More Jews came to Poland when Casimir the Great (1330-1370) gave them the right to buy or rent land anywhere in the kingdom.

Poland extended its boundaries to Lithuania and other provinces on the Baltic Sea, as well as to Galicia and the Ukraine on the Romanian border. Under the benign rule of the Polish kings, Jews settled in every corner of the land and established in the towns and villages communities called *kahals*. These kahals built schools and synagogues, set up courts of law, and established societies to care for the sick and poor. The Jewish craftspersons organized their own guilds. Jews leased and administered salt mines, became agents and overseers on the estates of the *pans*, and collected taxes from the peasants.

The Ukraine had once belonged to the Cossacks, a warlike people who had more in common with the aggressive Tartars than with the settled Poles. The Cossacks were of the Eastern Orthodox faith and resented being ruled by Roman Catholic Polish nobles and clergy. The Orthodox church was taxed, and the tax collector was often a Jew, who had the keys to the church and would not open it until the tax was paid. Oppressed by the Polish nobility, the Cossacks came to hate and resent their agents, the Jews.

This resentment flared up in the Cossack uprising of 1648. Led by their *hetman* (headman), Bogdan Chmielnicki, the Cossack raiders overran the Ukraine and the nearby provinces of Podolia and Volnynia. In rebellion against the Poles, they also vented their hatred against the Jews. They stormed into synagogues, slashed the holy arks, trampled on the scrolls, and set fire to the wooden structures. They mutilated, tortured, and killed the inhabitants of whole villages.

The Cossack wars continued, off and on, for seven years. During that time, between 300,000 and 400,000 Jews died, were driven out, or were sold into slavery to the Turks. The Chmielnicki

When Bogdan Chmielnicki (1595-1657) led the Cossacks of the Ukraine in an uprising against Polish rule, his followers killed thousands of Jews. Chmielnicki put the Ukraine under Russian protection in 1654. Ten years after his death, Russia and Poland divided the Ukraine between them.

massacres have been called the greatest disasters the Jews suffered until the time of Hitler.

These murderous raids also became part of the folk history of the Ukrainian Jews. A Jewish writer, Sholom Aleichem, was born 200 years later in the Ukraine but still noted the influence of the Cossacks on the culture of the area. In a story called "The Town of the Little People," he described a town which he called Kasrilevka and spoke of its old cemetery, rich in graves, which "They [the Jews] still value as they might a treasure, a rare gem, a piece of wealth. . . . For this is . . . the place where their ancestors lie, rabbis, men of piety, learned ones, scholars and famous people, including the dead from the ancient massacres of Chmielnicki's time."

The Jews of Poland who survived the Cossack massacres never regained the privileges they had enjoyed under the early Polish kings. Poland became involved in foreign wars and in civil strife and lost much of its territory and prestige in Europe. Outbreaks of violence against the Jews became common. Frightened and bewildered by the hostility of the people around them, the Jews shrank more and more from contact with the outside world.

Early in the 18th century, a religious revival occurred under a teacher named Israel ben Eliezer, who called himself Ba'al Shem Tov—Master of the Good Name. He founded a movement called Hasidism, which emphasized joy and enthusiasm in the worship of God. Hasidic Jews did not place primary emphasis on religious scholarship; instead, they maintained that even the uneducated common people could approach righteousness through simpler forms of piety. Hasidism did some good by revitalizing religious beliefs and making the hard lot of the people more bearable. Other movements that influenced Polish and Ukrainian Jews at this time were less benign. Some Jews fell prey to strange superstitions, began to believe in omens and evil spirits, and welcomed many self-appointed messiahs and miracle workers.

Out of the Ghetto

In 1648, the Thirty Years' War—a religious conflict involving most of the nations of Europe—ended. The Catholic and Protestant countries of western Europe then turned to rebuilding their ruined economies. With the passing of the feudal system, the religious persecutions of the Middle Ages had disappeared. The emphasis on economic development and the rational spirit of the age favored the Jews. The descendants of those who had once fled eastward began to return to western Europe.

Holland, which had received the Sephardic Jews earlier in the century, began to admit Ashkenazim from eastern Germany and Poland. Amsterdam became famous for its Jewish scholars, philosophers, and scientists, for its shipping merchants and experts in crafting fine jewelry from from gold and silver and precious stones. The Dutch masters painted Biblical subjects as well as scenes from contemporary Jewish life and portraits of noble Jews.

Portrait of a Rabbi *by Rembrandt van Rijn. Rembrandt often painted Jewish subjects.*

A group of Amsterdam merchants petitioned Oliver Cromwell, the Lord Protector of England, to lift the ban on the Jews. He complied not only for humanitarian but for practical reasons. The Jews had valuable international contacts, and the British needed their services.

Germany was still divided into a number of states, including a powerful kingdom called Prussia. Frederick the Great of Prussia (1712-1786) singled out certain Jews for favor and gave them special privileges such as the right to travel and to live in certain cities, like Berlin. These favored Jews helped to make Germany a great industrial nation by building textile

26

factories, railroads, and later electric plants. Many Jews distinguished themselves by their scholarship. Moses Mendelssohn, who had been born of a poor family in Dessau, came to Berlin and became the founder of the Jewish movement called the *Haskalah* or Enlightenment. He translated the five books of Moses into German, with a parallel text in Hebrew. From this text of the Bible, many Jews learned the German language.

Most of the German Jews, however, were still forced to live in ghettos. Strasbourg, a city in the Alsace-Lorraine region on the border of France and Germany, admitted Jewish peddlers only during the day. In the evening, a loud blast from a trumpet drove them back to their ghettos in outlying villages. Other towns in the Rhineland imposed on the Jews special taxes and limited their places of residence and occupations.

Among 18th-century philosophers, especially in England and France, a new emphasis on human rights became common. Such thinking inspired the leaders of the French Revolution, an event that had great impact on the living conditions of European Jews. In 1791, the French Assembly granted equal rights to the Jews of France. Even later, after Napoléon Bonaparte came to power in France, French troops were seen as liberators by Jewish communities in German or Austrian territories. When French soldiers marched into the cities of the Rhineland and Italy, they battered down the walls of the ghettos. As the ancient walls crumbled, martial bands played, fireworks were set off, and people—both Jews and their Christian neighbors—cheered and embraced each other.

The breaking down of the ghetto walls had a double result. It brought thousands of Jews, especially in France, into contact with the outside world and gave them a chance to enter trades and professions. At the same time it did away with some of the Jews' privileges of autonomy and self-rule. The Jews were now guided not by their rabbis and elders but by the law of the land. For instance, one of the rights granted by the French Assembly was the right to civil marriage. French Jews became French citizens first and Jews second. Later this happened in Germany as well. The German Jews considered themselves to be Germans "of Hebraic or Mosaic persuasion."

The Jews from Germany

Between 1820 and 1870, the population of the United States increased from about 10 million to about 39 million. Most of this growth was due to the great waves of immigration from central Europe, and especially from Germany. Because official immigration records listed the immigrants by the country they came from, not by their religion, it is hard to determine just how many of the immigrants were Jews. In 1820, there were between 4,000 and 5,000 Jews in America. By 1850, the number of American Jews had risen to between 40,000 and 50,000; by 1880, almost five times that many Jews lived in the United States.

The chief reason for this massive immigration to the United States from Europe was economic necessity. The population of Europe had grown tremendously in the early 19th century, and the Jewish population was growing even faster than the population as a whole. During the Industrial Revolution, which had started in England and spread to the continent, Christians and Jews alike from the countryside and small towns crowded into the cities in search of factory jobs. For those who could find work, this great displacement often meant dirty, dangerous work and crowded, unpleasant living conditions. For the many who could not find work, life was even harder.

Emigration from Europe seemed to offer a way out of poverty. The nations of the Americas—the United States in particular—seemed to offer what prospective emigrants wanted, especially land and jobs. Ocean travel was becoming more common, and thousands of Jews from Germany, western Poland, Austria, and Bohemia gathered in the Atlantic seaports—Bremen, Hamburg, Le Havre—and waited for passage to America.

Immigration societies were formed in Berlin, Vienna, and Prague to help the poorer immigrants. They traveled as steerage passengers, herded together among cattle and pigs, sleeping on wooden shelves arranged in tiers, eating food that was "hardly fit for cattle back in Bohemia," as one of the immigrants wrote in his diary. But the voyage lasted only a few weeks. After that came America, and the horizon was the limit.

The horizon lay to the west. Americans were crossing the mountains in covered wagons and staking out land in the western territories. The homesteads they left behind were taken over by German peasants, many of whom settled in Pennsylvania. German Jews settled among them, as they had in the old country. Others followed the wagon trails. Many of them—especially those who had never worked the land—did not know how to fell trees, plow farmland, or do many of the other things necessary to succeed on the frontier.

But the German-Jewish immigrants did not lack an adventurous spirit. Distance did not daunt them. They were willing to travel far, on foot if necessary, to endure hardships, to face loneliness. Most of the German Jews started out as peddlers, carrying baskets or packs filled with useful gadgets, cutlery, "notions" such as combs, scissors, needles, thread—anything and everything that the pioneers might need. Farm families living far from towns were accustomed to dealing with itinerant vendors and welcomed their coming. Quite often the settlers were European immigrants themselves and were glad to have a chance to talk to a peddler in their native language.

Some peddlers were more clever or perhaps luckier than others. They made enough money to buy a horse and buggy and a bigger stock of wares—perhaps farm implements, carpentry tools, pots and pans, and nice fabrics for clothing. If they came to a town or village that looked prosperous, they opened a general store, a hardware store, or dry goods business. In a few years they saved up enough money to send for their wives and children, for brothers and sisters. They wrote letters to Frankfurt, Strasbourg, or Posen and urged friends to join them in the new land. Others who were not so clever or lucky continued as itinerant peddlers or simply wandered the country in search of short-term labor. Their families back home perhaps never heard from them again.

The American Midwest and West attracted many German Jews. Cincinnati, Ohio, dates its first Jewish community from 1817; Louisville, Kentucky, from 1832; Chicago, Illinois, from 1842. Germans and German Jews came to Milwaukee and other cities in Wisconsin. Jewish immigrants followed the gold rush to California. In 1849, the year of the gold rush, a Yom Kippur service in San Francisco was held in a

Levi Straus sold denim pants that would eventually become an American classic.

tent. In western mining towns, Jewish merchants sold supplies to prospectors. The heavy denim pants called levis were first manufactured by a Jewish peddler named Levi Strauss in California.

In 1848, numerous revolutions broke out in Europe, but most failed—setting off a new wave of immigration. Many of the German Jews who came to this country after 1848 were intellectuals —teachers, writers, musicians—who did much to enrich the cultural life of America. Their struggle against European monarchy made them value American democracy and wish to preserve it. They joined the abolitionist

Judah Benjamin

Jews had been absorbed politically and economically into mainstream American life.

In the 19th century, many great American fortunes were made. Some of the fortunes, mainly in the retail business and to a smaller extent in manufacturing and banking, were made by Jewish immigrants from Germany who had started out as pack peddlers. Adam Gimbel and Benjamin Altman, for example, were peddlers who went on to establish large department stores in New York City.

Another of these success stories was that of Lazarus Straus, who came from Bavaria in 1854 and traveled through Georgia—first with a peddler's pack and then with a horse and buggy.

movement and fought for the Union during the Civil War.

But not all Jews were on the side of the North. Some who lived in the South favored the Confederacy. Judah P. Benjamin served under Jefferson Davis as secretary of war and secretary of state. Rabbi Isaac Mayer Wise of Cincinnati, a leader of the Reform Synagogue movement, sided with the South, and some rabbis preached sermons in which they attempted to prove from the Scriptures that slavery was morally acceptable. In opposition to them, Rabbi David Einhorn of Baltimore preached in favor of abolition—doing away with slavery. On the subject of slavery and states' rights, the Jews were as divided among themselves as were the rest of the American people. By the time of the Civil War, many

Rabbi David Einhorn

Benjamin Altman (**left**) *established a New York department store in 1906. Solomon R. Guggenheim* (**right**) *founded a major art museum in 1937.*

Straus eventually opened a shop in Talbotton, Georgia, and then sent for his wife and three small sons. After the Civil War, Lazarus Straus and his three sons—Isidor, Nathan, and Oscar—left Georgia and moved to New York City, where they opened a crockery business. In 1871, the Straus brothers rented a corner, where they diplayed china and glassware, in the basement of a store run by the R. H. Macy Company. By 1888, they had become partners in the Macy company, and, with imaginative merchandising skill, they turned Macy's into a huge department store. The Straus brothers were also noted for their many civic and philanthropic activities. Oscar Straus was ambassador to Turkey and secretary of commerce and labor under President Theodore Roosevelt. A member of the third generation, Jesse Isidor

Straus, once served as U.S. ambassador to France.

Baiersdorf, Bavaria, was the birthplace of the seven Seligman brothers, who began their business careers as peddlers in Alabama. Joseph Seligman was the first to come to America, in 1838, and his brothers followed him. In 1862, they moved from Alabama to New York and started a banking firm, which formed branches in New Orleans, San Francisco, Frankfurt, London, and Paris. Joseph Seligman was a good friend of General Ulysses S. Grant and a staunch supporter of President Abraham Lincoln. His firm obtained loans in Europe for the United States government and, after the war, continued to give financial support to the U.S. Navy. Joseph Seligman founded such organizations as the Hebrew Orphan Home. He was a member of the Board of Education in New York and president of the American Geographical Society.

Perhaps the most spectacular of the family fortunes was the one made by the Guggenheim family. The first member of the family to come to the United States was Meyer Guggenheim, who came from a small town in Switzerland where his family had lived for 200 years. In 1847, Guggenheim, who was then 19, began to peddle merchandise with a horse and buggy in the coal-mining towns of Pennsylvania. Later he manufactured lye and stove polish and sold imported Swiss embroidery. In the 1880s, he invested in some silver and lead mines in Colorado, then in copper mines and smelters. It was in copper that the Guggenheim fortune was made.

His sons expanded the business and became patrons of art, music, and the sciences. One of them, Simon, endowed the Guggenheim fellowships. Another, Solomon, founded the Guggenheim Museum in New York to house his collection of modern paintings and sculpture.

Religious and Community Life

In the European ghetto, the synagogue was not only a place of worship but also a house of study. The body of accumulated knowledge important to Jewish life was large. Besides religious doctrines and the history of the Jewish people, it included rules governing everyday conduct, philosophical discussions, parables, folk tales, legends, and poetry. A child could begin by learning the Hebrew alphabet, go on to reading the Bible, and continue to study and discuss the more difficult books such as the Mishnah. Prayers were an everyday obligation, which could be performed either in the synagogue or at home. The rabbi did not necessarily lead in worship. Rather he was a leader of the community, a teacher, and a judge. He would interpret the law and pass judgment on any question—from a divorce case or business dispute to a minute point of dietary law, such as whether a pot in which milk had been boiled could be used for cooking meat. He was also responsible for advising people and promoting the community's welfare.

Though the ghetto Jews paid taxes to European governments, they got almost no benefits in return. They were responsible for their own charities. Indeed, their religion laid this obligation upon them. The Hebrew word *zedaka* ("charity" or "benevolence") also means "justice." To provide for the poor, the sick, and the aged was simply an act of justice.

In America, Jews congregated less for self-preservation than for companionship. Jewish communities shared certain traditions, customs, and religious observances and wished to

A Jewish American observes the Sabbath eve in a cellar. Jacob A. Riis took this photograph in 1890.

preserve them. As immigration increased, Jews from a particular part of Europe tended to form little enclaves in America and to establish their own synagogues. By the time of the Civil War, there were between 50 and 60 synagogues in New York alone, representing German, Polish, Spanish, Dutch, Russian, English, and Bohemian Jews. Sometimes the members of one trade formed their own congregation.

The Jewish immigrants In America formed numerous *chevras*, or mutual

benefit societies. Some were quite small and perhaps had only one function, such as visiting the sick or providing an insurance or loan fund for its members. Others became social clubs as well, providing entertainment, literary discussion groups, choral societies, or orchestras. The young men's Hebrew literary societies of the 19th century gave rise much later to the Young Men's Hebrew Associations, patterned somewhat on the Young Men's Christian Associations (YMCAs) that had been founded in American cities. Other service organizations were also established so that Jews could assist one another. One of the largest was the Independent Order of B'nai B'rith, founded in 1843, which had lodges in many cities. By 1860, it had a membership of 50,000.

In the 1850s and 1860s, the German Jews began building hospitals in the larger cities. One reason for these hospitals was that Jewish patients who observed the dietary laws could not get kosher food in the general hospitals or those run by Christian denominations. Jewish orphanages and homes for the aged began to appear at that time.

Education had been a matter of concern for Jews ever since the time of

Hebrew Union College in Cincinnati, Ohio. Founded in 1875, it is the oldest rabbinical school in the United States.

the early settlers. The first synagogues tried to maintain schools for children, but separate Jewish school systems never became widespread. For the most part, Jewish-American children attended public schools, and the old synagogue schools dwindled and finally disappeared. In the 1860s, the last barrier to public-school education for Jews was overcome when schools no longer required attendance on Saturday, the Jewish Sabbath. For religious instruction, Jewish children went to voluntary Sabbath or Sunday schools (conducted in English) or to afternoon Hebrew schools that taught the Hebrew language and Jewish religious studies.

The first synagogues in America followed the Sephardic ritual, an Orthodox form of worship. In 1824, a group of 47 members of Beth Elohim congregation in Charleston, South Carolina, led by Isaac Harby, tried to institute some reforms in the ritual. They wanted to shorten the service, introduce English into the prayer book, and have the rabbi give a sermon in English. When the trustees of the synagogue refused this request, the reformers seceded and formed their own congregation. By the time they returned eight years later, a movement known as Reform Judaism had become influential in Europe and the United States.

The Jews arriving from Germany had been influenced by the Reform movement, which had started in Hamburg and Berlin. One of the innovations of that movement was the introduction of organ music. This was a hotly debated question, since the Orthodox synagogues had allowed only choral music. In the Orthodox synagogue, women sat in a separate section from the men, usually in the balcony. The men wore some sort of head covering and a prayer shawl. No part of the service was in the everyday local language (the whole service was in Hebrew), and there was no "sermon" in the modern sense of the word. Reformers argued that the Hebrew prayers were meaningless to many worshippers and that the whole ritual was antiquated.

In their zeal to modernize the ritual, they threw a great deal of it overboard. The Reform temples, as they were often called, were in many ways closer in appearance to some Protestant churches than to the old synagogues. The pillars, stained glass windows, choir lofts, organs, and sermons in English seemed alien to many Jews of more traditional leanings. Many Jews continued to worship in their accustomed fashion, or to make compromises between the old and the new. Over time, three organized branches of Judaism emerged—Reform, Conservative, and Orthodox.

3

THE JEWS FROM EASTERN EUROPE

Demonstrators in New York City in 1981 protested the Soviet government's restrictions on Soviet Jews. Many of America's Jews can trace their ancestry to Russia and other regions that became part of the Soviet Union.

Russia and the Jewish Pale of Settlement

In the latter part of the 19th century, when immigrants began pouring into the United States at an unprecedented rate, the second largest single group (next to the Italians) were the Jews from eastern Europe. They came from a broad area. Thousands came from Romania and the Austrian province of Galicia. By far the largest number, however, came from Russia—or, to be more exact, from the Jewish Pale of Settlement in the Russian Empire.

This Pale of Settlement had existed only since the latter part of the 18th century. In earlier times, few Jews had lived in Russia proper. Only rarely were Jewish merchants from Poland and Germany allowed temporary entry to the great Russian trading fairs. Even

Peter the Great (1682-1725), who imported German, Dutch, and English shipbuilders, stonemasons, mechanics, and merchants to help him modernize his backward country, excluded the Jews. Russia in the 18th century was a feudal country with an autocratic czar, a powerful Eastern Orthodox church, a small landed nobility, and millions of serfs working the land.

At the close of that century, Catherine the Great of Russia expanded her empire by annexing most of Poland and other territories. One million Jews lived in the Ukraine, the Baltic countries, and Poland. At practically one stroke, they became Russian subjects. What was to be done with them? The czarina, Catherine, solved the problem by defining a boundary beyond which Jews could not go. This border area in which the Jews were confined became known as the Jewish Pale of Settlement.

The czars who followed Catherine the Great—Alexander I, Nicholas I, and Alexander II—kept shifting their policies in respect to the Jews. At times the pale was enlarged, then it was restricted again. A decree would order the Jews to leave the rural areas and move into the towns. Then the decree would be revoked. Jews were allowed to have homes in some towns, but in others a Jew needed a special permit simply to enter. A permit might be good for only 24 hours, and any Jew caught out of bounds had to pay a fine. Russian officials, however, were usually open to bribes, and the Jews learned to live with a corrupt government.

Before the establishment of the pale, the Jews had their own self-governing bodies or *kahals*. These kahals were now stripped of all their powers except that of collecting taxes—and the taxes imposed on the Jews were twice as high as those for other groups. The government policy toward education also kept shifting. Nicholas I had a minister who argued that the only way to absorb the Jews was to educate them. For this purpose "crown" schools were established.

At first the Jews welcomed such schools, but only until it became obvious that the main function of these schools was not to educate Jews but to convert them to Christianity. The Russian government then ordered the Jews to select rabbis to conduct government business—issue birth certificates, perform marriages, officiate at funerals, settle legal disputes. These were called "crown rabbis," and—since they were puppets of the government—they were extremely unpopular with the people. Resenting such government intrusions, most Jews stubbornly maintained their own schools, went to their own rabbis for advice and the settling of disputes, and organized their own welfare societies.

The government intrusion that was hardest for Jews to ignore was compulsory military service. In Russia during the early 19th century, men

The Jewish Pale of Settlement in the late 19th century encompassed 16 provinces west of the Russian heartland. These provinces included the Ukraine and parts of Poland.

had to serve in the army for 25 years. A cruel law by any standards, it had an additional, barbaric feature in the case of the Jews. Jewish boys were conscripted at the age of 12 instead of 18, and they had to spend six years in a "cantonment" in order to be indoctrinated into the Eastern Orthodox faith before they began their 25 years of military service. Parents whose sons were taken into service mourned them as dead. Even if a man survived the brutal life of the army camps and did not die on the battlefield, he came out after 31 years a complete stranger to his own people. Jews did not send their children willingly, but gangs of chappers (kidnappers) roamed the countryside and snatched children away to hand them over to the government. If a rumor said that a gang of kidnappers had been seen, parents hid their boys in the woods or even had them crippled or maimed.

In 1855, during the reign of Alexander II, the 25-year term of service was changed to 6 years and the "canton-ment" was done away with. It seemed to the Jews that a new and better day was dawning. When Czar Alexander II freed the serfs in 1861, Russians— including the 3 million Jews in Russian territory— rejoiced. They felt that the new czar was truly a liberator.

This was not entirely the case. When 47 million serfs were set free, their masters were compensated for their loss, but the serfs themselves were not given any land. They only swelled the great mass of landless, impover-ished Russian *muzhiks* (peasants) who lived in squalid huts together with the pigs and cattle. They could neither read nor write, and most of them be-lieved anything the village priest chose to tell them.

Alexander II and his advisers, like the German rulers a century before, were astute enough to see that the Jews could be useful. The laws were relaxed in some cases to allow the wealthier Jews and those who quali-fied as skilled mechanics to establish residence in Moscow and a few other cities in Russia. The crown schools were abandoned, and a certain num-ber of Jewish students were allowed to enter the regular *gymnazia* (high schools) and universities. A Jewish professional class came into existence— doctors, lawyers, teachers, engineers. Some studied in England or Germany and came back with liberal ideas.

In 1863, Jews took part in an un-successful Polish rebellion. Political

"criminals" were exiled to Siberia. Others left the country. But most of the Jewish people were not affected. Political rebellion at that time was a luxury for the educated and compara-tively well-to-do. Most of the Jews simply wanted to be left alone.

Village Life

The typical Jewish village or small town of the Russian Pale differed from the 16th-century ghettos of western Europe. It was not enclosed by a stone wall, but it was set off from the rest of the world by an invisible barrier made up of folk customs, religious observ-ance, and a close-knit community and family life. Most of the people were poor. They worked as cobblers, tailors, carpenters, glaziers. A few kept taverns or small shops. Someone who had nei-ther a trade nor a shop might travel about the countryside with a horse and wagon or even on foot to seek odd jobs. Such laborers seldom traveled so far that they could not get back to their families before the Sabbath.

The Sabbath began on Friday after sundown. No matter how poor a fam-ily was, even if it lived on potatoes and cabbage all week, some coins were set aside to buy fish or meat and a white loaf for the Sabbath dinner. The men hurried to the synagogue for eve-ning prayer. The women, who had scrubbed and cooked during the day, now lit the Friday-night candles. Up and

Jewish boys attending a cheder, or elementary Hebrew school. The melamed's elderly father is seated at the left.

down the narrow streets, from every window these candles glimmered. The inviting smell of cooking filled the house. There was a saying that a person could starve any day of the week, but nobody ever starved on the Sabbath. Even the town's paupers and tramps, who slept on synagogue benches and lived on handouts, were assured of one hot meal during the week. It was an honor to share the Sabbath meal with a guest. If a stranger arrived in town or was stranded during a journey (traveling was forbidden on the Sabbath), he or she went to the synagogue knowing that someone would offer hospitality.

Families were large, often with three generations living under one roof. Marriages were arranged by the parents of young people, often with the help of a professional matchmaker. Very often the betrothed couple did not see each other before the wedding. "Time enough to get acquainted later," the old people said in jest, which was tinged with sadness. They knew that life would be hard. There was hardly such a thing as a carefree time of youth. In Jewish law divorce was allowed, but it was not very common. The birth of a child was a happy occasion, and small children were tenderly cared for. But school began early, at the age of five, sometimes sooner. Boys were sent to *cheder* (elementary Hebrew school) where they studied from early morning until dark with little free time for play. The *melamed* (teacher) was expected to exercise strict authority, enforced with slaps if necessary.

Though the countryside was not far away, Jewish children seldom went swimming or fishing or roaming in the woods. Some of the holidays, however, brought nature to them. During the fall holiday *Sukkoth*, every family built its own little *sukkah* (hut) and decorated it with branches and autumn fruits.

Piety and learning were held in highest regard, more than wealth. A young man who devoted himself to studying the Torah and Talmud might have a father or father-in-law who supported him and his family. Often his wife earned the family living. Many women not only managed their households and raised their children but also operated a business of some kind, perhaps a tavern or shop. Women were not given a voice in community affairs and they sat apart from the men in the synagogue, but they were respected and honored in the family circle. This was during a time when other Russian women were considered their husbands' property and when domestic violence against women was not even illegal.

The traits that characterized the Jews of the Pale of Settlement—a willingness to work hard and subsist on little, loyalty to family ties, regard for learning, rigid piety, and a moral obligation toward life—came with the Jews to the New World.

The Immigrants

Alexander II was assassinated in 1881, and his successor, Alexander III, took stern measures to crush any hint of rebellion. The various nationality groups within the Russian Empire—Polish, Latvian, German—were forbidden to use their native languages in the schools. Strict censorship was imposed on books and newspapers. Loyalty to "Mother Russia" became the watchword, and Mother Russia was synonymous with the czar's government. To deflect criticism from the government and the church, village priests and officials blamed the Jews for many of the hardships of Russian life. Bloody massacres, or *pogroms*, broke out against Jews throughout the Pale of Settlement. After the turn of the century, armed gangs called "The

Black Hundreds" marched against Jewish villages with religious banners, portraits of the czar, and the cry, "Down with the Jews!"

In May 1882, the czar issued a set of rules, which became known as the "May Laws." These complex laws were intended to break up the Jewish villages and small towns and to relocate the Jews to larger towns, which were already badly overcrowded. Jews were not allowed to settle anew in another village, even if they had inherited property in it or wanted to join their families. Local authorities were given the right to expel any Jews they did not want and to seize their homes. In some places, the Jews were allowed to produce something but not to sell it. Thousands lost their means of livelihood. Schools and universities changed their admissions policies so that it was almost impossible for a Jew to enter a Russian school. Jewish lawyers were not admitted to the bar.

In 1891, the Grand Duke Sergei became governor of Moscow and ordered all the Jews leave the city at once.

Russian Jews are expelled from their home village, 1881.

A rare photograph shows young Jewish revolutionaries gathered by the body of a friend killed in the Kishinev pogrom of 1903.

Between 15,000 and 20,000 Jews in Moscow were forced out of town under police guard. Where would all these displaced people go? As one of the czar's ministers, Constantin Petrovich Pobedonostsev, cynically remarked, one third would die, one third would leave the country, and the rest would become absorbed into the general population and lose their identity as Jews.

At least one part of his prediction came true. Hundreds of thousands of destitute and desperate people began leaving the country. They were granted exit permits, but since these required long waits and bureaucratic red tape, many crossed the borders secretly at night. They streamed into the border towns of Germany and Austria. The Jews of these countries became dismayed at the masses of refugees, hungry, ragged, and often ill from exposure, who looked to them for assistance. The German Jews at first tried to stem the tide, to plead with these people to go back. They sent delegations to the czar to intercede on their behalf. When fresh pogroms broke out, such as the Kishinev pogrom of 1903, heads of foreign governments, including President Theodore Roosevelt of the United States, sent notes of protest to the czar. The protests were ignored. The Jews of western Europe began helping the refugees. The *Alliance Israelite Universelle*, which had been formed a few decades before to help victims of cholera epidemics, now sent committees to the border towns to help the refugees with money, clothing, and medical care.

The Russian Jews spread throughout western Europe and England. Many then sailed overseas to South America, South Africa, and Canada. For most of the displaced Jews, however, the ultimate goal was the United States of America, and most of those who found their way to the United States landed at New York.

Before they could be allowed into the United States, the newly arrived immigrants had to undergo an examination at Ellis Island in New York harbor. To people weary from the long journey and distrustful of government officials, this was a terrifying ordeal. Organizations such as the Hebrew Immigrant Aid Society (HIAS) sometimes provided interpreters and helped the immigrants in other ways. If they passed the physical examination and successfully answered a long list of questions, the immigrants were allowed to enter the United States and face the challenge of life in a strange new land.

New York's East Side

The saying was, "In America people rake up gold in the streets." The immigrants did not believe this as a literal fact, but even as a symbol it was no longer true. By the 1880s, the limitless horizon was gone. The frontier had been settled, and America had become more urban. The new Jewish immigrants, instead of setting out on the road with a peddler's pack, congregated in the large cities—New York, Philadelphia, Boston, Chicago. A few had the dream of "going back to the land," and joined cooperative farming communities in South Dakota, Oregon, and other states. Except for a few cooperatives in New Jersey, these idealistic projects did not last long. Most of the Jews who arrived in New York City stayed there.

The reasons for staying in New York were simple. Unlike many other immigrants to America, Jews commonly came not individually but in families. The ratio of women and children to men among the Jewish immigrants was higher than in other groups. With children to care for, the Jews quickly had to find work and a place to stay.

On the East Side of New York City, many Jews found work as cigar makers,

Moe Levy & Co., a clothing factory in New York, about 1912

garment workers, and pushcart peddlers. A dignified old man with a beard and skullcap who had sat over the Torah in his native town in Russia might be seen selling pretzels on Hester or Rivington Street. Another Jew might spend 17 hours a day bending over a sewing machine or pushing a heavy steam iron back and forth across a pressing board. Young girls worked in crowded factories that were drafty in winter, stifling in summer, and filled with dusty, polluted air all year round. Men earned between $6 and $10 a week, women and girls between $4 and $5. This type of work was called "the sweatshop system."

It was not really a system at all, since it had grown up in a haphazard fashion. Earlier in the century, most clothing had been custom-tailored or sewn at home. The invention of heavy sewing machines and steam presses, together with an increased demand for ready-to-wear clothing, created a thriving garment industry. Because starting a garment factory was less expensive than getting into other forms of manufacturing, earlier Jewish immigrants from Germany entered the business. By the latter part of the 19th century, these German Jews owned most of the garment factories in New York City.

The owners of garment factories, instead of carrying out the whole manufacturing process, divided it up among various contractors. The factory owners employed skilled cutters who cut out the garments on their premises, then sent the bundles of cuttings to the contractors, who in turn hired workers to do the basting, sewing, pressing, and finishing. The contractors rented a loft in a rickety building or used their own tenement flats as shops, crowding machines and workers into every available corner. If the workers complained, they were told to leave. Plenty of fresh immigrants came off the ships every day to take the place of anyone who annoyed a shop supervisor.

Every now and then, a catastrophe would draw public attention to the appalling conditions in the sweatshops. One of the worst occurred on March 25, 1911, when a fire broke out at the Triangle Shirtwaist Company, which employed mostly young girls. Several girls jumped to their death from a seventh-floor loft, and 144 died in the fire. Later, the states began enacting safety legislation, but the workers themselves also began to organize unions. The unions eventually convinced the owners of sweatshops to reduce the work week to 40 hours, raise wages, and improve working conditions.

The labor movement had been growing all over the United States, in a wide variety of industries. In 1881, several craft unions joined together under the leadership of Samuel Gompers, a Jewish cigar-maker from London. By 1886, this association had evolved into the American Federation of Labor. The "needle trades," as the garment trades were sometimes called, went through a long trial-and-error period until they formed two giant trade unions.

In 1914, the workers in men's clothing formed the Amalgamated Clothing Workers of America. Sidney Hillman became president of this union in 1915 and held that post until his death in

Sidney Hillman

1946. In the 1930s, Hillman also helped found of the Congress of Industrial Organizations (a federation of many labor unions), and he was one of President Franklin Roosevelt's close advisers.

The other great union, the International Ladies' Garment Workers Union (ILGWU), was founded in 1900. In 1910, the ILGWU took part in a strike, called the Great Revolt, that lasted two months, involved 60,000 workers, and resulted in a history-making settlement called the Protocol of Peace. This settlement was negotiated by Louis D. Brandeis, a Jewish Boston lawyer who later became a justice of the U.S. Supreme Court. The Protocol for Peace established an arbitration board, grievance committees, and other innovations that later became standard practice in labor-management relations.

The two great unions of garment workers pioneered other approaches to help their members as well. They had a system of unemployment insurance before the federal government took over that function. They also built low-cost housing, established health centers, nurseries, and summer camps, operated adult-education classes, and presented lectures and concerts.

One musical production, *Pins and Needles* (with book by Marc Blitzstein and songs by Harold Rome and others), was put on with a cast made up entirely of garment workers of the ILGWU in 1937. It included songs of social protest, such as "Sing Me a Song of Social Significance," as well

*A scene from **Pins and Needles**, 1937. All the actors are garment workers.*

as catchy boy-meets-girl love songs. Planned originally as a weekend entertainment for union members, it made stage history by playing on Broadway for three years and becoming more successful than any previous musical.

The People's Speech

To the immigrant Jews, Hebrew, the language of ancient Palestine and of modern Israel, held a special significance. It was the language of the Bible, the Talmud, and the book of prayer. The everyday speech of most European Jews, however, was not in Hebrew.

Over the course of centuries, the Jews had learned the languages of the countries to which they migrated. The Sephardim, besides speaking Spanish, used a language that was a mixture of Spanish and Hebrew and was written in Hebrew characters. This was called Ladino. In the Middle Ages in Germany, the Jews began speaking the local dialect—Middle High German. Again, they mixed Hebrew words with it and wrote it in Hebrew characters. This was the language they brought with them to eastern Europe. Since the German word for Jew, *Jude*, became *Yid* in eastern Europe, the language was called *Yiddish*. In Poland and Russia, the language acquired many Slavic words, but it remained basically Germanic.

For many centuries in Europe, the Yiddish language was not held in high esteem. Scholars and serious writers wrote their books in Hebrew, just as medieval scholars had written in Latin, scorning the everyday languages of their day. But a vernacular, or everyday language, becomes stronger and richer with use. This is what happened to Yiddish. At first it was considered suitable only for informal verses, light romances, and folk tales. It became a literary language late in the 19th century, when writers began using it for lyric poetry, plays, stories, and novels. Its former drawbacks became its virtues. Since it was a mixture to begin with, Yiddish was very flexible, and it easily incorporated new words and phrases.

Because Yiddish had been used by ordinary people—laborers, peddlers, and vagabonds—it had a strong, earthy quality. What it lacked in grammatical complexity it made up in a varied vocabulary. Though it had been lightly dismissed as "kitchen talk," it was not trivial. Yiddish was the language in which mothers and fathers sang lullabies to their children. Older Jews used Yiddish to talk about the old days in the little European towns, about flights and pogroms, about sons who had been kidnapped into the army or had run off to America. Used in so many deeply meaningful situations, the language had a strain of tenderness and melancholy. It also had wit and a wry kind of humor.

As the immigrants began learning English, they mingled English words and phrases with their Yiddish. Those Jews who were born in America spoke English almost exclusively. But, even as the everyday use of the Yiddish language declined, Yiddish words and phrases cropped up on the stage, in novels, on radio, and on television. Some Yiddish words—such as *schmooze*, *schmear*, and *chutzpah*—have even become widely used among non-Jewish Americans.

The Yiddish Press

In an era when newspapers were numerous and highly competitive, the Yiddish-language press was as lively as the rest. At one time there were 12 Yiddish papers published in New York alone, and their combined circulation was probably more than half a million.

Yiddish weeklies and monthlies began to appear during the 1870s, and the first daily paper came out in 1885. This daily, called the *Yiddishes Tageblatt* (Jewish Daily News), was probably the first Yiddish daily in the world and lasted 43 years before it merged with other papers. The Yiddish papers reflected every shade of political opinion, from the conservative and religion-oriented *Yiddishes Tageblatt* and *Morning Journal* (established in 1901) to the Zionist *Day* (1914), the socialist Jewish daily *Forward* (1897), the communist *Freiheit*, and even a few small anarchist papers. These papers carried on a constant rivalry among themselves, not only in print but in arguments among the editors, writers, and intellectuals who gathered in the East Side cafés to drink tea and discuss the issues of the day.

Though printed in Yiddish, the only language many of their readers knew, the papers were far from parochial or narrow. Their aim was to educate the new immigrants and to help them adapt to life in the United States. Besides national and international news, they printed articles on American government and history, instructions on how to become naturalized citizens, news about unions, clubs, and fraternal organizations, and articles on popular science. Every paper printed letters from readers asking for advice on domestic problems. Of these the *"Bintel Brief"* ("Bundle of Letters") section of the Jewish daily *Forward* became the best known. The Yiddish dailies and weeklies devoted more space to literature than English-language newspapers usually did. They printed—often in daily installments—translations of European and American classics and novels by Yiddish writers. Among the working people in the ghetto there were many self-taught poets and writers who contributed poems, short stories, and essays dealing with the everyday lives of the immigrants. Well-educated Jewish journalists produced high-quality reviews of books and plays.

The front page from an 1897 edition of the **Forward.** *In the cartoon, Czar Nicholas II, surrounded by bodies, tries to strike a bargain with Uncle Sam.*

Among the Yiddish journalists, Abraham Cahan (1860-1951) stands out. He had graduated from a teachers' institute in Vilnius, Lithuania, and taught elementary school for a short time, until his participation in revolutionary activity made it difficult for him to remain in Russia. He came to New York in 1882 and worked at various odd jobs—as a cigar maker, a teacher, the editor of a small weekly paper—until he helped found the *Forward* in 1897. He left this paper to work for an American newspaper, *The Commercial Advertiser*, but returned in 1902 as editor and built up the *Forward* into a great newspaper with a circulation of 200,000 at its peak. Cahan was deeply concerned about the problems of the sweatshop workers, and he did a great deal, both as an editor and as a speaker, to help the unions. Cahan also wrote and published stories and novels in English. In 1917, he published *The Rise of David Levinsky*, which has become a classic of Jewish immigrant life.

The Commercial Advertiser, on which Cahan worked for several years, was a lively, crusading New York paper edited by Lincoln Steffens, who later became known for his books exposing corruption and graft in big-city politics. At the *Advertiser*, Abraham Cahan met and became friendly with a young writer, Hutchins Hapgood. When Hapgood was assigned to write a series of sketches about the Jewish immigrants of New York's East Side, Cahan acted as his guide and interpreter. Cahan introduced him to old Hebrew scholars, fiery young Russian radicals, laborers and shop clerks, artists and actors and writers. Hutchins Hapgood's sketches, under the title *The Spirit of the Ghetto*, were published in book form in 1902 and reprinted in 1967. Hapgood's writing was accompanied by portraits of East Side characters sketched by a young Jewish artist named Jacob Epstein. At the time of his collaboration with Hapgood, Epstein lived and worked in the garret of a tenement overlooking Hester Street, in the heart of the ghetto. Epstein later moved to England, where he became a renowned sculptor and was knighted.

The Yiddish Theater

The favorite form of entertainment among East Side Jews was the theater. The early Yiddish theater was not always serious and intellectually challenging. Most of the truly popular productions were melodramas, vaudeville acts, light operas based on Biblical and historial subjects, sentimental sketches, or broad farces. Later,

The Grand Street Theatre on New York's Lower East Side, about 1900

under the influence of serious playwrights and such actors as Jacob Adler and Maurice Schwartz, a realistic element was added and plays attempted to depict the true life of the ghetto.

Whatever the play was—tragedy, comedy, or farce—the audience participated. They laughed, cried, hissed, cheered, and applauded the actors. On weekend nights, whole families turned out, including children. During intermissions they bought souvenirs and refreshments, talked with old friends and met new ones. In its popular appeal, the Yiddish theater resembled the Elizabethan theater of William Shakespeare's day.

The history of the Yiddish theater has been traced to the synagogue ritual. Many Jews considered the theater —because it used costumes and masks —to be a form of idol worship, but most Jews loved music, especially vocal music. In the synagogue, the service was conducted by a cantor, who sang or chanted the prayer, with emphatic intonations, while the congregation made a rhythmic response. Some European cantors had developed a highly individual style, and people came a great distance to hear them. Such a cantor was young Sigmund Mogalesco, the cantor at the Bucharest synagogue. He had been a child prodigy, had traveled through Romania and southern Russia, and at the age of 14 had led a choir of 20 men.

In 1876, a musician named Abraham Goldfaden heard Mogalesco sing and

Sigmund Mogalesco

decided that the young cantor had not only a remarkable voice but a talent for acting. Goldfaden was a Russian Jew with a talent for writing and singing. After he failed in business, he became a sort of music-hall performer; he wrote poems, set the words to popular tunes, and sang in Romanian taverns. Goldfaden wrote a play and persuaded Mogalesco, who was then

52

20, and several members of the synagogue choir to make up the cast. The play was an immediate success, and the troupe began touring various towns in Romania and Russia.

In 1883, the Russian government outlawed the Yiddish theater on the pretext that it was a hotbed of political intrigue. Goldfaden's theater troupe then immigrated to New York, where Goldfaden managed to base his operations in a rented theater that he called the Rumania. Other acting groups arrived from Europe and performed in such theaters as the Germania, the People's, the Windsor, and the Thalia. Forgetting the old Talmudic injunction against idol worship, the theater lovers almost worshipped their favorite actors. One of the matinee idols of the day was Boris Thomashefsky, a dark, handsome, rather heavy-set man with curly black hair and a simpering manner who played romantic leads. (The European-bred audiences preferred their stars, both male and female, to be on the plump side.)

To satisfy the growing demand for shows, playwrights turned out plays by the hundreds, often borrowing from

The front page of some of the sheet music from an adaptation of William Shakespeare's **King Lear.**

53

novels and other plays. Shakespearean works were popular on the Yiddish stage, both in straight translation and in adaptions. There were Yiddish versions of *Hamlet* and *Othello* and a Jewish *King Lear*. *The Doll's House*, a classic by the Norwegian playwright Henrik Ibsen, had a Jewish counterpart in a play called *Minna*, originally written by Leon Kobrin and later revised by Jacob Gordin. Gordin also wrote *God, Man, and the Devil*, an adaptation of Johann Goethe's *Faust*. After the turn of the century, Jewish playwrights were producing original plays based on Jewish life and folklore. In the 1920s, there were 12 Yiddish theaters in New York and several in other large cities, as well as numerous touring companies. They produced a number of excellent actors, some of whom later distinguished themselves in non-Jewish theater.

Food

In the Jewish neighborhoods of New York and other large cities, distinctively Jewish restaurants, bakeries, and delicatessens were founded. Like other immigrants, the Jews wanted to continue enjoying favorite foods from their home countries.

Many Jewish foods originated in central or eastern Europe. For example, blintzes (thin, folded pancakes filled with cottage cheese) are related to Russian blini. Borscht, a soup made of beets and served cold with sour cream, is a variant of Russian *borshch* or Polish *barshch*. Buckwheat kasha (*kasha* means "cereal") and buckwheat pancakes come from eastern Europe, where buckwheat was cultivated. Other Jewish favorites from Europe are knishes (baked pastry filled with chopped meat, mashed potatoes, or a mixture of both), kreplach (triangle-shaped dumplings filled with cheese or chopped meat and served in soup), and another type of dumpling called knaidlach.

Bagels—doughnut-shaped hard rolls that are boiled before being baked—were introduced to America by Jews but have become widely popular among non-Jews as well. Many people spread cream cheese on bagels. Others eat them with lox, which is smoked salmon.

All kinds of fish—salted, pickled, and smoked—appear in Jewish delicatessens, a type of food store that Jews have made a part of American culture. Delicatessens—often known simply as delis—sell prepared, ready-to-eat foods such as sandwiches, cold meats, and salads. In Jewish neighborhoods, however, delicatessens offer not only convenience but also an outlet for food prepared according to the rules of Judaism.

In Jewish neighborhoods, many delicatessens and butcher shops bear the word *kosher* on their signs. This means that the foods sold there conform to *kashruth*, Judaism's dietary code.

Some meats (such as pork) are *treif*, or forbidden. Other meats, such as beef and chicken, can be eaten, but only if the animals from which the meat comes have been slaughtered in the proper way by a *shochet*, someone trained to process meats in the manner required by Judaism. Some parts of cattle, like the hind legs, are not eaten, but liver and tongue are kosher. Shellfish, incidentally, are not kosher. In addition, an old Biblical injunction not to "seethe a kid in its mother's milk" is interpreted to mean that milk or milk products, such as cheese and butter, should not be eaten along with meat.

Limited as they were by these rules, Jewish cooks had to use considerable ingenuity in preparing their food. Since many of them had to be frugal as well, they used materials that were cheap and plentiful, such as dried beans, peas, lentils, root vegetables, and dried fruits. A dish made of meat with carrots, or meat with potatoes and prunes, is called a *tzimmes*. Cooks experimented with this dish by adding various ingredients and flavorings, and the word *tzimmes* became part of a slang phrase. When someone wanted to say, "Don't exaggerate," or "Don't make a mountain out of a molehill," he or she might say, "Don't make a whole tzimmes out of it."

The Jewish holidays all have their special foods. Passover celebrates the escape of the ancient Jews from Egyptian bondage. Since the fleeing Jews had no time to wait for their bread to rise, they ate flat cakes of unleavened bread. This is the *matzo* which is eaten instead of bread during the days of Passover. At the *seder*, or Passover supper, a plate with symbolic foods is placed on the table. It contains horseradish to symbolize the bitter days of bondage; *charoseth* (a mixture of chopped apples, nuts, and wine) for the mortar that went toward the building of the pyramids; a bone of the paschal lamb; and a sprig of parsley or other green vegetable to denote hope and the coming of spring.

Purim celebrates the feast of Queen Esther and the downfall of Haman, the enemy of the Jews. Cookies filled with prunes or poppyseed and shaped like triangles to represent Haman's hat are called *hamantaschen*. On Friday night, which ushers in the Sabbath, Jews traditionally have a large braided loaf of white bread (the *challah*), a bottle of wine, and gefilte fish (a type of fishball) accompanied by red or white horseradish.

Assimilation Begins

In the large cities, welfare organizations formed by Jews of German descent and settlement organizations in slum areas worked hard to "Americanize" and "civilize" the immigrants. Often welfare workers making their rounds found that the people they were trying to "civilize" had already been skillfully blending their own rich and meaningful culture into the American mainstream.

This was especially true of the children of immigrants. When a family arrived from Europe, the older children often had to work to help support the family, while the younger children went to public school. Both at work and in school, the children learned the new language and new customs fast—too fast, it seemed to their parents. They played in the street with other children (often of Italian or Irish descent), picked up American slang, and adopted a whole new folklore that was incomprehensible to their parents. In Hebrew school, the children had been taught to admire the heroes of Jewish history—the Maccabees and Simon Bar Kochba. Now they had a whole new set of heroes—prize-fighters and baseball players. In the synagogue they chanted the sacred music; in the street they picked up the tunes of Tin Pan Alley and American jazz. To this popular culture many Jews made a significant contribution.

As the economic lot of the immigrants improved, their children stayed in school longer, and more Jews went on to high school and college. Even before World War I, the sons and daughters of east European Jews were beginning to enter professional fields. This Americanization of Jewish immigrants also blurred the once-sharp line between the Jews from Germany and those from eastern Europe.

Anti-Semitism

For about 300 years, America had maintained an open-door policy toward European immigration. When 16 million people arrived from Europe within three or four decades, however, this policy was challenged. Organized labor objected on the grounds that the immigrants threatened jobs. The white-collar urban people had a vision of the cities being filled with slums. Farmers and small-town people in the West and South heard hateful speeches assuring them that the Anglo-Saxon America was being swallowed up by inferior people from southern and eastern Europe. After the 1917 Russian Revolution, anti-immigrant hysteria swept the country, and eastern Europeans were viewed as revolutionaries with bombs in their pockets.

In 1921, the United States Congress passed a law that severely restricted immigration. According to this law, the number of new immigrants from any country could be no higher than 3 percent of the foreign-born persons of that group already in the United States. The number already in the United States was determined according to the 1910 census—a count that did not include the many immigrants from southern and eastern Europe who had immigrated since 1910. In 1924, the Johnson-Reed Immigration Act limited the number of new immigrants even further—to only 2 percent of the foreign-born of any given nationality

A pushcart peddler on the Lower East Side of New York

already in the U.S. as of 1890. These immigration laws almost put a stop to immigration from southern and eastern Europe. What Congress was saying, in effect, was that Italians, Slavs, Jews (and most non-Europeans) were less desirable than the people of northern Europe.

Anti-Jewish attitudes had long been a problem in Europe and North America. (Such attitudes are often called anti-Semitism, because the Jews belong to the Semitic language-culture group.) Because the Jews were different from the majority of people in Europe and America, some outright nonsense about Jews became widely believed. For example, *many people accepted a ridiculous story that, in 1913, a Jew named Mendel Beiliss had killed a Christian child in Russia and had used the child's blood for baking the Passover matzos. (Beiliss was tried for murder but was found innocent.)* In America, anti-Jewish feeling ran high during a 1915 murder case in Atlanta, Georgia. Leo Frank, a Jew and a northerner, owned a factory in Atlanta. He had been accused, on flimsy evidence, of having killed a 14-year-old girl. He was sentenced to death, but Georgia's governor commuted the death sentence to imprisonment. Incensed by this easing of Frank's sentence, a mob dragged Leo Frank out of prison and lynched him in Marietta, Georgia.

Modern anti-Semitism derived from many sources. In the late 19th and early 20th centuries, many books published on both sides of the Atlantic claimed that northern peoples were superior to peoples—like the Jews—of more southerly origins. Also, a new movement called Populism arose in the 1890s among the farmers of America's Midwest who were crying out for agrarian reforms. The Populists had a genuine grievance, but they blamed their troubles on an imaginary conspiracy against them in the big cities —New York and London—by "Jewish and English bankers." The leading Populist hero was William Jennings Bryan, a candidate for president of the United States who, in the 1896 campaign, made his famous "Cross of Gold" speech. This speech implied a link between the execution of Christ and the betrayal of the farmer by the bankers.

In the 1920s, anti-Semitism took on a more concrete form. Henry Ford published in his paper, *The Dearborn Independent*, a series of anti-Semitic articles. Some of these were later collected in a four-volume publication under the title *The International Jew*. Part of Ford's writing was a supposed transcript of a document known as "The Protocols of the Elders of Zion." This document had a curious history. It had first been "discovered" and publicized at the turn of the century in Russia by the czar's secret police. It was supposed to be the transactions of a group called the Elders of Zion, who had met in Prague and had plotted to take over the governments of the world with the help of corrupt politicians, Freemasons, liberals, and atheists. There had never been such a group or such a conspiracy. Several American and Swiss courts declared that the "Protocols" document was a fake (rulings ignored by Nazi agents who used it in Switzerland). Henry Ford had to disclaim it, but the document was revived briefly by the Ku Klux Klan and again discredited.

Between 1920 and 1930, the Ku Klux Klan, a racist organization formed just after the Civil War, was revived, with a new anti-Jewish agenda. In the 1930s, a severe economic depression made Americans desperate enough to listen to various anti-Semitic organizations and individuals. Father Charles Coughlin, a Catholic priest, used his newspaper *Social Justice* and his weekly radio broadcasts to blame the ills of society on "international Jewish bankers and radicals." He was eventually silenced by the Catholic church itself. During the years before World War II,

Father Charles Coughlin

58

THE
INTERNATIONAL
JEW

THE WORLD'S
FOREMOST PROBLEM

Being a Reprint of a Series of Articles
Appearing in The Dearborn Independent
from May 22 to October 2, 1920

PUBLISHED BY
THE DEARBORN PUBLISHING CO.
DEARBORN, MICH.

NOVEMBER, 1920

Aspects of Jewish Power
in the
United States

Volume IV
of
The International Jew
The World's Foremost Problem

A Fourth Selection of Articles from
THE DEARBORN INDEPENDENT

Published by
The Dearborn Publishing Co.
Dearborn, Mich.

May, 1922.

Title pages from some of Henry Ford's anti-Semitic tracts, which spread false claims that an international Jewish conspiracy threatened America.

discrimination was practiced against Jews in housing and employment. Many companies made no secret of the fact that they did not hire Jews. Certain neighborhoods were off limits to Jews who wanted to rent or buy homes. Many universities and colleges adopted a quota system that limited the number of Jewish students.

Hitler's rise to power in Germany and his attacks against the Jews had their echoes in America. The German-American Bund, with Fritz Kuhn at its head, held meetings that were smaller-scale versions of the anti-Jewish rallies in Nazi Germany. Local hate groups patterned themselves on anti-Semitic European groups such as the fascist Black Shirts and the Nazi Brown Shirts. They made speeches, circulated anti-Semitic books and pamphlets, and looked to their local *führers* to start a real assault on the Jews. When President Franklin Roosevelt initiated his New Deal policies to revive the U.S. economy, he was sharply criticized because some of his advisers happened to be Jews.

The attack on Pearl Harbor and the declaration of war on Nazi Germany dispersed the local Nazi groups and dealt a most effective blow against organized anti-Semitism. Jews in all walks of life fought in the war along with Americans of every national origin—including German and Japanese. When the war ended in 1945 and the enormity of what Hitler had done to European Jews became known, a feeling of revulsion against Nazi ideas and methods turned the tide of anti-Semitism. Six million Jews had been killed. The realization that anti-Semitism could be carried to such a conclusion in modern times shocked most Americans.

Golda Meir, born in Russia, was raised in Wisconsin and eventually served as prime minister of the state of Israel (from 1969 to 1974).

Zionism

Although many Jews had found a refuge and a new home in the United States, others continued to cling to the centuries-old dream of a Jewish homeland in Palestine. The establishment of a Jewish homeland was the chief goal of the movement called Zionism. The modern Zionist movement got its start in the 1880s, when some Russian Jews formed an organization called the Lovers of Zion and began setting up small Jewish colonies in Palestine. The movement continued to develop under the leadership of Theodor Herzl (1860-1904), a Hungarian Jewish scholar who was worried by the increasing anti-Semitism he saw in Europe. In 1896, Herzl published the book *Der Judenstaat* (The Jewish State), which called for the establishment of a Jewish nation.

The following year, the First Zionist Congress was held in Basel, Switzerland. The congress developed a program with three main goals: to create a Jewish state in Palestine, to organize Jews throughout the world, and to seek the help of other countries in founding a Jewish homeland.

The early 20th century brought many political changes in Palestine, and by the end of World War I, the area was under the control of Great Britain. In 1917, the British government issued the Balfour Declaration supporting the establishment of a Jewish state in Palestine. This policy was actually made a part of the international agreement authorizing Great Britain to govern Palestine. Such an arrangement, however, was strongly opposed by the Arabs living in Palestine. To help quell Arab unrest, the British government began in the 1920s to discourage further Jewish immigration to Palestine.

After World War II, militant Zionists launched a campaign to force the British government to allow a Jewish state in Palestine. The problem was submitted to the United Nations, which decided in 1947 to partition Palestine into an Arab state and a Jewish state. The following year, the state of Israel was established.

As a movement, Zionism did not end after the Jewish state came into existence in 1948. The money and effort that had gone into the establishment of Israel was now needed to support the new nation. In later years, the dangers posed by Israel's hostile neighbors made continued support necessary.

Israel's flag is hoisted for the first time at United Nations headquarters, May 12, 1949.

4
CONTRIBUTIONS TO AMERICAN LIFE

Kapelye is one of about 100 bands in North America that have rekindled interest in **klezmer,** *the traditional dance music of the Jews of eastern Europe.*

The scope and importance of Jewish contributions to American life are staggering. In nearly every field of endeavor, from government to the sciences to the arts, American Jews have taken the lead and have demonstrated exceptional talents.

Government and Public Affairs

Among the many Jews who have held positions in the United States government, some of the most prominent have served on the Supreme Court. The first Jew to be appointed to the Court was Louis D. Brandeis (1856-1941), who became an associate justice in 1916 and served until 1939. As a member of the Court, Brandeis wrote many decisions supporting social legislation. Benjamin Cardozo (1870-1938) was another liberal jurist concerned with social issues. He was appointed to the Supreme Court in 1932 and served until the time of his death. In 1939, President Franklin D. Roosevelt named Felix Frankfurter (1882-1965) an associate justice of the Court. Born in Vienna, Frankfurter was a professor of law at Harvard when he received his appointment. During his 23 years on the Supreme Court (1939-1962), he was noted for his independent decisions and his concern with individual rights.

In the executive branch of government, American Jews have been influential as cabinet members and presidential advisers. President Franklin Roosevelt's friend and neighbor from New York State, Henry Morgenthau, Jr., served as Roosevelt's secretary of the treasury from 1934 to 1945, initiated the successful wartime drive for Victory Bonds, and was an advocate of worldwide monetary reform. David Lilienthal was director and chair of the Tennessee Valley Authority from 1933 to 1941 and served as chairperson of the Atomic Energy Commission from 1946 to 1950. Anna Rosenberg, an expert in labor and personnel relations, held positions with several government agencies during the New Deal years and was assistant secretary of defense in the Truman administration from 1950 to 1953. Financier Bernard Baruch acted as an adviser on economics and national defense to every president from Woodrow Wilson to John F. Kennedy.

A noted Chicago labor lawyer, Arthur Goldberg, served as secretary of labor

Arthur Goldberg

under President Kennedy in 1961. The following year, Goldberg became an associate justice of the Supreme Court. He resigned from the Court in 1965 to take a post as U.S. ambassador to the United Nations, a post he held until 1968. In 1970, after serving two years as president of the American Jewish Committee, Goldberg ran unsuccessfully for governor of New York. President Jimmy Carter appointed

Arthur Burns

first scientist to head the Department of Defense. From 1979 to 1981, Neil Goldschmidt, the former mayor of Portland, Oregon, was secretary of transportation in Carter's administration. Alfred Kahn, an economist from Cornell University who had been one of President Dwight D. Eisenhower's economic advisers, was chosen by President Carter in 1978 to head the Council on Wage and Price Stability and to find ways to fight the nation's growing inflation. Kahn had earlier served as chairperson of the Civil Aeronautics Board (from 1977 to 1978), where he helped bring about lower airline fares. Another economic adviser, Arthur Burns, resigned from service in 1978 after eight years as chair of the Federal Reserve Board, which sets the nation's money policy.

Goldberg in 1977 to be the U.S. envoy to the Conference on Security and Co-operation in Europe.

Henry Kissinger, a Harvard professor of political science, was appointed by President Richard M. Nixon to the National Security Council in 1969 and became Nixon's chief policy adviser. In 1973, the German-born Kissinger was appointed secretary of state, a post he held until 1977. For his efforts to bring an end to the Vietnam War, Kissinger was awarded the Nobel Peace Prize in 1973.

In 1977, President Jimmy Carter appointed Harold Brown as secretary of defense. Brown, a physicist and expert on nuclear weapons, was the

In 1932, Democrat Herbert Lehman succeeded Franklin D. Roosevelt as governor of New York. He served until 1942 and in 1949 was elected to the United States Senate. Lehman remained active in politics after his retirement in 1956, leading a reform movement within the Democratic Party of New York City. Another Democrat, Ernest Gruening, was appointed governor of the Alaska Territory in 1939. He campaigned for statehood and served as one of Alaska's first senators, from 1959 and 1968. In 1961, President Kennedy appointed Abraham Ribicoff, then governor of Connecticut, as secretary of health, education, and welfare. Ribicoff served one year in that position and then was elected to the United States Senate in 1962. Ribicoff retired in 1981.

New York City, which has the largest population of Jewish Americans in the country, elected its second Jewish mayor in a row in 1978. Edward Koch, a former representative from Manhattan to the U.S. House of Representatives, succeeded Abraham Beame in the job of grappling with the problems of one of the largest urban areas in the world.

In 1990, 8 members of the U.S. Senate and 31 members of the U.S. House of Representatives identified themselves as being Jewish. These legislators are part of a strong tradition of political involvement among American Jews. As a congressperson from 1946 to 1954 and as a senator from 1956 to 1980, Jacob Javits, a Republican from New York, was one of the most liberal Republicans in Washington. He was one of the major backers of the 1964 Civil Rights Act. Representative Elizabeth Holtzman of New York gained prominence in 1974, when she served on the House Judiciary Committee, which held hearings into charges against President Richard Nixon. After leaving Congress, she became Kings County (New York) district attorney. Another high-profile representative from New York, Bella Abzug, served in the U.S. Congress from 1970 to 1976 and was appointed to lead the National Advisory Committee for Women in 1978. Early in 1979, President Carter

Walter H. Annenberg, a publisher and patron of the arts, was U.S. ambassador to Great Britain from 1969 to 1974.

fired her from that post because of a disagreement over federal policy. Senator Warren B. Rudman, a Republican from New Hampshire, led the Senate campaign in the 1980s to reduce federal budget deficits.

Business and Industry

American Jews have been prominent in many industries and have founded and operated some of the largest commercial concerns in the United States. Many Jewish Americans continue to work in fields—such as retailing and the garment industry—that were the

65

specialties of Jewish immigrants in the late 19th and early 20th centuries. Other businesses, however, have also been significantly shaped by the efforts of Jewish Americans. One of those in which they have been most influential is the publishing field.

A Yiddish-language press still exists, even though its reading public has dwindled. Several book publishers specialize in Yiddish and Hebrew books as well as English-language books oriented toward the Jewish reader. The oldest of these is the Bloch Publishing Company, founded in 1854 in Cincinnati by Edward Bloch and Rabbi Isaac Wise. From Cincinnati it moved to Chicago and then to New York. Another company specializing in Jewish books, the Jewish Publication Society, was established in Philadelphia in 1888.

Jewish influence in American publishing, however, goes far beyond the area of Jewish specialty books. In 1915, Alfred A. Knopf established the publishing company bearing his name, a company that published works by many Nobel Prize-winning authors from around the world. Bennett Cerf—who later became a well-known writer and humorist and appeared on the television game show *What's My Line*—founded the Random House publishing company 1925.

In the late 19th century, several newspapers were rescued and given new life by two noted publishers. Joseph Pulitzer (1847-1911), who was half

Joseph Pulitzer

Jewish, came to America from Hungary in 1864. He combined two papers to form the *St. Louis Post-Dispatch* and then moved on to the *New York World*. He also established a school of journalism at Columbia University and endowed the Pulitzer Prizes, which have been awarded since 1917. In 1896, Adolph Ochs (1858-1935) went to New York from Chattanooga, Tennessee, and became the publisher of *The New York Times*, then on the verge of bankruptcy. Over the next 40 years, Ochs developed it into one of the world's greatest newspapers.

William Zeckendorf, a Jewish-American real-estate developer, had a role in the construction of the United Nations building in New York City. When he heard that the United Nations was looking for a permanent home, he proposed to the site-selection committee that they consider a parcel (formerly the site of some slaughterhouses) owned by Zeckendorf's company. Zeckendorf accepted an offer of $8.5 million from the United Nations, and the next day John D. Rockefeller—an extremely wealthy industrialist whose son Nelson was on the site-selection committee—offered to donate to the U.N. the full purchase price of the property.

The Jewish-American Levitt family was also highly influential in the real-estate business. Abraham Levitt, whose parents had emigrated from Russia, was in business with his sons William and Alfred when the U.S. housing industry entered one of its greatest boom periods. When American soldiers returned home after World War II, an acute need for new, inexpensive housing developed. The Levitt firm responded by building two huge suburban developments—one on Long Island in New York (in 1947) and another in Pennsylvania (in 1951). Both of these communities bore the same name, Levittown, and they offered only one style of house. A later Levittown, built in New Jersey in the 1960s, offered three styles of house. Although the Levittowns have been criticized for their lack of variety, they were very successful, they served an obvious need, and they attracted many willing buyers.

Several people of Jewish ancestry have made their mark on the cosmetics and fashion industries. Diane von Furstenberg is well known for her ready-to-wear dresses and several other products bearing her name, including cosmetics and wallpaper. Vidal Sassoon first came to public attention as an influential hair stylist and later created a line of popular hair-care products that bear his name.

In 1975, Irving S. Shapiro became chairperson and chief executive officer of E.I. du Pont de Nemours & Company, one of the largest chemical companies in the United States. Shapiro was also influential as one of President Jimmy Carter's chief advisers on business affairs.

Science

From the earliest times, Jews have valued the art of healing. Before medicine became the science it is today, European kings consulted Jewish doctors, and two of the Marranos with Columbus were doctors.

The names of diseases or their cures are often derived from the names of the scientists who have discovered these diseases or cures. Salk polio vaccine is named for Dr. Jonas Salk, a Jewish researcher who developed the

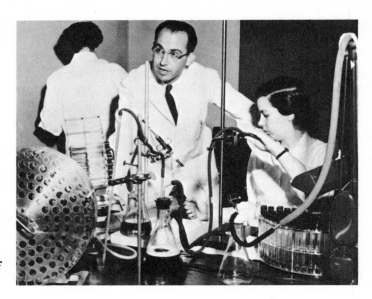

Jonas Salk, developer of the Salk polio vaccine.

first highly effective vaccine against paralytic poliomyelitis. In 1975, he founded the Salk Institute for Biological Studies. Flexner B. dysentery was named for Dr. Simon Flexner of the Rockefeller Foundation, who isolated the cause of that disease in 1889. He also conducted experimental studies of diphtheria toxins and discovered a treatment for victims of spinal meningitis.

A Jewish doctor who pioneered in preventive medicine was Joseph Goldberger (1874-1929). Born in Austria, he came to the United States at the age of six. After graduating from Bellevue Hospital Medical School in New York, he entered the U.S. Public Health Service in 1899 and was sent to Cuba and Mexico, where he studied yellow fever and typhus. Between 1913 and 1925,

he made a study of pellagra—a disorder of the intestines and nervous system—among poor people in the South. It was thought at that time that pellagra was caused by a germ, but Dr. Goldberger demonstrated that this disease was caused by an inadequate diet. His findings laid the basis for the modern science of nutrition.

Dr. Selman A. Waksman (1888-1973), working with a team of research scientists in soil chemistry at the New Jersey Agricultural Experiment Station, isolated streptomycin—only the second antibiotic to be discovered (the first was penicillin). He originated the name *antibiotics* for this and similar substances. Streptomycin, effective against many diseases, was especially valuable against tuberculosis, once a widespread disease that was almost always fatal. For this discovery and for subsequent work with other antibiotics, Dr. Waksman received the Nobel Prize in physiology and medicine in 1952.

In 1921, the Nobel Prize for physics was awarded to Albert Einstein (1879-1955). Einstein, whose theories of relativity are among the greatest scientific advancements of modern times, was a German Jew, but he had gone to Switzerland as a young man and did most of his important scientific work there. In 1914, he returned to Germany to become physics research director of the Kaiser Wilhelm Physical Institute in Berlin. Einstein held that position until 1933, by which time he recognized that the rise of the Nazis in Germany presented a grave threat to German Jews. In 1934, he came to the United States to head the school of mathematics in the Institute for Advanced Study at Princeton, New Jersey, where he taught and worked until his death in 1955.

Another Nobel Prize winner in physics (1944) was Isaac Isidor Rabi, who received the prize for his work in phenomena related to magnetic fields. Rabi was born in Austria in 1898 and was brought to the United States as a child. During World War II, Rabi did research in the field of microwave radar. From 1952 to 1956, he was a member of the General Advisory Committee of the Atomic Energy Commission. Much of his research concentrated on the peaceful uses of atomic energy, and

he was one of the founders of an international laboratory at Geneva, Switzerland, for the study of high-energy physics.

A number of Jewish-American physicists were involved in the development of the first nuclear weapons. The most prominent among them were Edward Teller and J. Robert Oppenheimer. Teller worked on the research team that developed the first atomic bomb, and later he led the U.S. push to develop a vastly more powerful weapon—the hydrogen bomb. Born in Budapest, Hungary, in 1908, Teller received a doctorate from the University of Leipzig and worked as a research associate at

Selman Waksman

J. Robert Oppenheimer

Oppenheimer, whose father was a German-born textile manufacturer, was born in New York in 1904. He graduated from Harvard in 1926 and later studied in Europe. Between 1929 and 1947, he taught at the University of California and at Cal Tech and did research in theoretical physics. In the 1930s, Oppenheimer was deeply disturbed by the events in Nazi Germany —Hitler's persecution of Jews—and by the depression in the United States (which made it hard for many of his

the University of Göttingen. Teller then lectured at the University of London until 1935, when he emigrated for the United States. After World War II, Teller became deeply suspicious of the Soviet Union's military plans. Although many scientists and politicians opposed developing the immensely destructive hydrogen bomb, Teller managed to win the necessary support in Congress. America's first fully usable hydrogen bomb was tested successfully in March 1954—by which time the Soviet Union had already successfully tested its own hydrogen bomb. Later, Teller became a strong advocate of President Ronald Reagan's Strategic Defense Initiative—a system of satellites intended to destroy incoming missiles before they could hit U.S. targets.

Edward Teller

students to find jobs). During this period, many intellectuals, scientists, and artists who were also concerned about these problems took part in left-wing political movements. Though Oppenheimer did not join any leftist political party, he had friends who did.

In 1943, Oppenheimer was appointed director of the nuclear research laboratory at Los Alamos, New Mexico, where he headed a team of scientists and technicians who succeeded in detonating the first atomic bomb. After the war, from 1947 to 1952, he was chairman of the General Advisory Council of the Atomic Energy Commission (AEC). Along with several other scientists disturbed by the destructive potential of nuclear weapons, he refused to work on the hydrogen bomb. This refusal prompted the AEC, in December 1953, to publicly question Oppenheimer's loyalty to the United States. Oppenheimer's friendship with members of the Communist Party and with other leftists was offered as evidence of disloyalty. When his case was formally heard in 1954, Oppenheimer was cleared of disloyalty charges. Nonetheless, he was stripped of his high security clearance and was not allowed to continue to work with the AEC.

J. Robert Oppenheimer served as director of the Institute for Advanced Study at Princeton from 1947 until shortly before his death in 1967. In December 1963, the AEC partially reversed its earlier insult to this great physicist by presenting him with the $50,000 Fermi Award, the AEC's highest public honor.

Art

In 1905—the year in which the Autumn Salon of Paris first exhibited works by Paul Cezanne, Henri Matisse, and other progressive artists snubbed by the staid French Academy of Art—a young American artist named Max Weber arrived in Paris. Max Weber (1881-1961) was the son of Russian-Jewish immigrants who had come to America when he was 10 years old. Although his family was poor, Weber managed to study art at the Pratt Institute in Brooklyn before going to Paris. Weber remained in Paris for three years and studied with Matisse. When he returned to America, Weber brought with him the revolutionary art concepts and techniques he had learned in Paris. In his early paintings based on New York scenes, Weber demonstrated a free and dynamic use of form and color. His painting *Chinese Restaurant* (1915), owned by the Whitney Museum of American Art, is often reproduced as an example of American abstract art. Later in his career, Weber's work became representational and he turned for subjects to his Jewish background. Examples of this work are *The Hasidic Dance* (1940) and *Adoration of the Moon* (1944). The latter is derived from an old Jewish ceremony in which

10 men at the close of the Sabbath gather in the courtyard of the synagogue to bless the rising moon when its light is the strongest.

Mark Rothko (1903-1970), an abstract painter, was at one time a student of Weber's. Rothko was born in Russia and came to the United States at the age of 10. His work received considerable attention after his suicide in 1970, and many of his paintings nearly doubled in value. As a result, they became the focus of lawsuits by Rothko's heirs against art dealers who were handling his work. Rothko's paintings hang in two New York museums, the Whitney and the Museum of Modern Art, and in the Chicago Art Institute. A major retrospective exhibition of his abstract paintings began at New York's Guggenheim Museum in 1978 and then toured the country.

Aaron Bohrod, another Jewish-American artist, emphatically opposed the abstract forms that Rothko painted. Instead, Bohrod aligned himself with the regional school of American painters. Born and raised in Chicago, he said that he wanted to do for Chicago what John Sloan had done for New York—that is, paint city streets, houses, and railroads, whether they were conventionally beautiful or not. Appointed artist-in-residence at the University of Wisconsin, he also painted the towns and countryside of the Midwest, as well as scenes from the West and South. Later in his career, he also worked on pottery and textile design.

Hyman Bloom and Jack Levine, both of Boston, painted expressionist works—rich in texture, brilliant in color—that are represented at the Whitney, the Museum of Modern Art, and other leading American art galleries. Bloom used Jewish subjects, such as cantors, rabbis, and synagogue interiors. Jack Levine's paintings depicted avarice, greed, and violence in modern society. Two examples are *Gangster's Funeral* (1952) and *The Trial* (1956).

Ben Shahn (1898-1969) was an artist of remarkable range and versatility, whose work included fresco murals, oil paintings, and watercolors, as well as posters and book and magazine illustrations. The son of a carpenter, he was born in Lithuania and was brought to New York at the age of eight. As a young boy in Brooklyn, he did sidewalk chalk drawings of the sports heroes of the day. He attended high school at night and worked during the day as a lithographer's apprentice. His work as a lithographer gave him a thorough knowledge of draftsmanship. One of the first books he illustrated—with border illustrations and a hand-lettered text—was a *Haggadah*, a Hebrew book of the Passover service. In the 1930s and 1940s, he, along with many artists, worked for the Federal Arts Project. He painted fresco murals for government buildings—the Bronx Central Annex Post Office, the Farm Security Building in Washington, D.C., and a housing development for garment workers in Roosevelt, New Jersey.

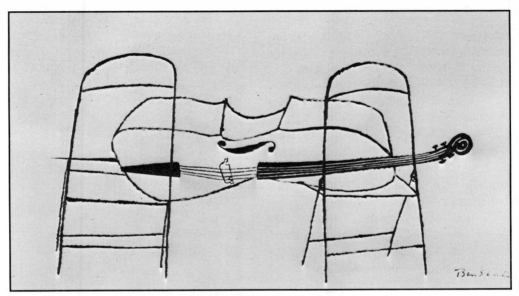

Cello with Chairs *by Ben Shahn*

Literature

Many Jewish-American novelists have drawn on their Jewish backgrounds to create classic fiction. Among them are two winners of the Nobel Prize in literature—Saul Bellow and Isaac Bashevis Singer.

Saul Bellow was born in Lachine, Quebec, and grew up in Chicago. Several of his works are set in Chicago, including a comic novel for which Bellow won a National Book Award—*The Adventures of Augie March* (1953). Two of Bellow's other works, *Herzog* (1964) and *Mr. Sammler's Planet* (1969), also won National Book Awards. In these later, more serious novels, Bellow portrays Jewish characters reacting to the violence and alienation of modern American life. Another of Bellow's novels, *Humboldt's Gift*, was awarded the Pulitzer Prize for fiction in 1976, the same year that Bellow received the Nobel Prize. Some of Bellow's later novels were *A Theft* and *The Bellarosa Connection*, both published in 1989.

Isaac Bashevis Singer, who won the Nobel Prize in 1978, was born in Poland in 1904 and came to the United States in 1935. The author of numerous short stories, novels, and books for children, Singer writes in Yiddish and has his works translated into English. Many of Singer's stories depict Jews living in Poland between the two world wars. The Nobel Prize committee described his work as "art which, with roots in a Polish Jewish cultural tradition, brings universal human conditions to life." Among Singer's best-known books are *Gimpel the Fool* (1957), *The Magician of Lublin* (1961), *In My Father's Court* (1966), *A Crown of Feathers* (which won a National Book Award in 1974), and *Shosha* (1978). Two of Singer's books—*Enemies, A Love Story* (1972) and *Yentl, the Yeshiva Boy* (1983)—eventually were adapted for the cinema.

A number of other outstanding American writers have drawn on their own experiences as Jews in writing their novels and short stories. In the 1930s, Michael Gold and Henry Roth wrote fictional accounts of Jewish immigrant life in New York City. J. D. Salinger, Bernard Malamud, and Philip Roth have all produced highly regarded fiction about Jewish Americans. Joseph Heller's novel *Good as Gold* (1978) describes an American Jew who seeks to escape his identity and become a part of the Washington bureaucracy. Other Jewish-American novelists who have written on Jewish subjects include such popular writers as Herman Wouk, Leon Uris, Leo Rosten, and Chaim Potok.

Jewish-American writers have also produced high-quality nonfiction about Jews in America. Early in the 20th century, Mary Antin, the daughter of Jewish immigrants, wrote about her own experiences in *The Promised Land*. Later autobiographical works by Jews include three volumes by the

Isaac Bashevis Singer

literary critic Alfred Kazin—*A Walker in the City* (1951), *Starting Out in the Thirties* (1965), and *New York Jew* (1978). Irving Howe's *World of Our Fathers*, which gives a historical account of Jewish immigrant life on the Lower East Side of New York during the early 20th century, won the National Book Award for history in 1977.

American Jewish writers have not confined themselves to Jewish subjects. Fiction writers such as Nathaniel West, Dorothy Parker, Edna Ferber, Jacqueline Susann, Erich Segal, Irving Wallace, and Erica Jong have dealt with themes ranging from fantasy to

Saul Bellow

romance to the problems of modern life. Isaac Asimov is one of America's leading writers of science fiction and of popular science books, with more than 400 titles to his credit. In another area, three of the most popular American novels about World War II were written by Jewish authors—*Catch-22* (1961) by Joseph Heller, *The Young Lions* (1948) by Irwin Shaw, and *The Naked and the Dead* (1948) by Norman Mailer. Mailer is noted not only for his novels but also for works that use fictional techniques to describe current history. In this category is his book *Armies of the Night*, which won both a Pulitzer Prize and a National Book Award in 1969. Other Jewish nonfiction writers include biographer Irving Stone, historian Barbara Tuchman, and feminist Betty Friedan, whose book *The Feminine Mystique* (1963), played a major role in the growth of the women's liberation movement. Jewish-American humorists such as S. J. Perelman and Art Buchwald have produced some of the finest satire of the the 20th century. Many American Jews—such as Lionel and Diana Trilling, Philip Rahv, and Leslie Fiedler—have also distinguished themselves as literary critics. Film critic Pauline Kael, who has written reviews for *The New Yorker* magazine since 1968 and has contributed to numerous other publications, is also a Jewish American.

Music

In the 19th-century villages of the Russian Pale, fiddlers were looked down upon as frivolous, uncouth characters. Somewhat ironically, however, many of the great violin virtuosos of the 20th century were Russian Jews. Among them were Mischa Elman, Jascha Heifetz, and Nathan Milstein, all of whom later immigrated to the United States. World-famous violinist Yehudi Menuhin was born in New York City in 1916 and began playing when he was only four. At the age of seven he made his solo debut with the San Francisco Orchestra, the start of Menuhin's career as a master of the violin.

Jewish-American musicians have also occupied an important place on the opera stage. Tenors Richard Tucker and Jan Peerce had long careers as performers with New York's Metropolitan Opera. Before his debut at the Met in 1941, Tucker was a cantor in Brooklyn. Beverly Sills, born Belle Silverman in Brooklyn in 1929, became one of the opera's top sopranos. She began singing with the New York City Opera and performed in more than 70 different operas. Her fame spread when she appeared on television specials and, later, developed her own television interview program. In 1975, Sills made her belated debut at the Metropolitan Opera. Four years later, she retired from singing in order to become a director of the New York City Opera.

Many other Jews have contributed to the history of 20th-century music. Aaron Copland—who, in his music for such ballets as *Rodeo*, *Billy the Kid*, and *Appalachian Spring* brought a uniquely American touch to symphonic compositions—was a Jewish American,

as were such other pioneering composers as Arnold Schoenberg, Darius Milhaud, George Gershwin, and Leonard Bernstein. Violinist Isaac Stern, pianists Vladimir Horowitz, Artur Rubinstein, and Rudolf Serkin, and cellist Gregor Piatigorsky have demonstrated their musical talents before concert audiences around the world. Clarinetist Benny Goodman performed with several symphony orchestras, but his greatest impact was as a consummate jazz musician. Goodman, known as the King of Swing, not only was a great soloist but also led one of the top jazz bands of the 1930s and 1940s.

In the 1960s, a revival of folk-oriented popular music owed much to talented American Jews—particularly Bob Dylan, Paul Simon, and Art Garfunkel. Bob Dylan (born Robert Zimmerman in Hibbing, Minnesota) capitalized on his rough voice and simple guitar work to build a reputation as a rebellious critic of the establishment—both musical and political. Many of his early songs— such as "The Times They Are A-Changin'," "Blowin' in the Wind," and "A Hard Rain's A-Gonna Fall"—have become classics of the folk-rock genre. Dylan was also known for abrupt changes in his musical and philosophical directions. Forays into country music and highly electrified rock were not unusual for Dylan, but he attracted even more attention when he converted from Judaism to Christianity in the late 1970s. Dylan then gravitated back to Judaism in the mid-1980s.

Irving Berlin (above) and George Gershwin (below), two of America's greatest composers. Among Berlin's best-known songs is "White Christmas." Gershwin's compositions ranged from lighthearted show tunes to symphonic pieces.

Musicians Paul Simon and Art Garfunkel also introduced folk songs that became American classics—"The Sounds of Silence," "Bridge over Troubled Water," "Homeward Bound," and many others. In the 1970s, Simon and Garfunkel ceased to issue albums as a duo, and each pursued other interests. Garfunkel continued to record, but much of his attention was devoted to an acting career that included well-received performances in such films as *Catch-22* and *Carnal Knowledge.* Simon, by far the more influential musician of the two, issued several successful solo albums in the 1970s and 1980s, including the Grammy Award-winning *Graceland* album (1986) —which contributed greatly to the international popularity of black South African music. In 1990, Simon experimented with West African and Brazilian rhythms in his album *Rhythm of the Saints.*

In 1911, a song called "Alexander's Ragtime Band" was all the rage. It had been composed by Irving Berlin, a Jewish American born in Russia in 1888 and originally named Israel Baline. Berlin came to New York as a small child with his family. (His father was a part-time cantor in a synagogue, and his older brothers worked in sweatshops and sold newspapers.) At the age of nine, after his father died, Irving Berlin left home and earned his keep by leading a blind singer around the saloons of New York's East Side. After working for a short time as a singing

Violinist Isaac Stern

waiter, Berlin began composing songs for Broadway musical revues and plays. During a long and productive career, Berlin wrote the music for such classic musicals as *Annie Get Your Gun* and composed some of America's best-known songs, including "White Christmas."

Besides Irving Berlin, numerous Jewish-American composers have essentially defined the Broadway musical genre. Jerome Kern, George Gershwin, Richard Rodgers (with Lorenz Hart and Oscar Hammerstein), Frederick Loewe (with Alan Jay Lerner), Jerry Bock (with Sheldon Harnick), and Leonard Bernstein have all created Broadway classics. Bernstein (1918-1990), a versatile composer and symphony conductor, was one of the most influential figures in American music during the middle and later 20th century. His *West Side Story* (1957) won acclaim and contained many individual songs, such as "Tonight" and "Maria," that became American standards. Bernstein also gained a reputation for his books and television shows that explained symphonic music in terms that non-musicians could understand.

The influence of Stephen Sondheim on the American musical theatre has been substantial. Both a lyricist and a composer, Sondheim created such musicals as *A Funny Thing Happened on the Way to the Forum* (1962), *Company* (1970), *A Little Night Music* (1973), and *Sweeney Todd* (1979). Even though many critics believed that, by the 1970s, Broadway musicals could no longer draw large audiences, Sondheim's shows proved otherwise. He also composed the songs that Madonna sang in the movie *Dick Tracy*—songs that also appeared on Madonna's 1990 album, *I'm Breathless*.

Another important theatrical composer of Jewish heritage, Kurt Weill, was well known in Europe before he came to the United States in 1935. Born in Germany in 1900, Weill wrote the music to such popular works as *The Threepenny Opera* (with text by the German playwright Bertolt Brecht), which opened in 1928 at a small theater in Berlin. It ran for five years and was popular throughout Europe during the 1930s. Although it appeared briefly on Broadway in 1933, no really expert English-language version of the play was staged during Weill's lifetime. (He died in 1950.) Then Marc Blitzstein, a notable composer, introduced a new version of *The Threepenny Opera* in March 1954, the beginning of a long off-Broadway run. Blitzstein's score features the popular song, "Mack the Knife."

Theater, Films, and Television

In the 1920s the American theater was enlivened by many playwrights of Jewish origin, among them George S. Kaufman, Moss Hart, S. N. Behrman, Elmer Rice, and Sidney Kingsley. In the 1930s, Clifford Odets wrote plays of social protest. *Awake and Sing!* was about a Jewish family caught in the hard times of the Great Depression. *Golden Boy* told the story of an Italian youth who was forced by poverty to turn from music to professional prizefighting.

Lillian Hellman, a native of New Orleans, first came to public attention in 1935, when her play *The Children's Hour* was produced. She is best known for *The Little Foxes*, a play about the changing South which was made into a film and an opera. Hellman wrote three books describing her life and literary career—*An Unfinished Woman* (1969), *Pentimento: A Book of Portraits* (1973), and *Scoundrel Time* (1978). Another serious Jewish-American playwright is Arthur Miller, who wrote the classic drama *Death of a Salesman* (1949). Miller, who was married to actress Marilyn Monroe from 1956 until 1961, also wrote *All My Sons*, *The Crucible*, and *A View from the Bridge*. Working in a lighter style, Jewish-American playwright Neil Simon wrote such successful comedies as *The Odd Couple* and *Barefoot in the Park*.

The Marx Brothers: (from left to right) Groucho, Harpo, and Chico

Many Jewish Americans have become well known not so much for writing comedy as for presenting it—in the movies, on television, in small comedy clubs, and on lavish stages in Las Vegas. Many Jewish comedians got their start in clubs in the borscht belt, a nickname given by *Variety* magazine to the summer resorts in New York's Catskill Mountains. (These resorts attracted many Jewish vacationers and featured favorite Jewish foods, such as borscht.) Jewish-American comedians like the Marx Brothers, Danny Kaye, Zero Mostel, Jack Benny, Sid Caesar, Milton Berle, and George Burns were some of America's most successful entertainers. Other Jewish comics—such as Rodney Dangerfield and Roseanne Barr Arnold—have continued this tradition of great American comedy.

Jewish-American performers in award-winning films have been numerous. Judy Holliday received an Academy Award in 1950 for *Born Yesterday*, re-creating a role she had originated on Broadway. Shelley Winters, a two-time Oscar winner, was named best supporting actress in both 1959 (for *The Diary of Anne Frank*) and 1965 (for *A Patch of Blue*). Actress and singer Barbra Streisand won an Oscar in 1969 for her performance in the title role of *Funny Girl*, a musical film based on the life of the Jewish American entertainer Fanny Brice. In 1977, Richard Dreyfuss was named best actor for his role in *The Goodbye Girl*, an original screenplay written by Neil Simon.

Al Jolson, a Jewish American born in Lithuania in 1886, starred in *The Jazz Singer* (1927), the first major "talking" motion picture. Later films featured such Jewish-American stars as Edward G. Robinson, Lee J. Cobb, Howard Da Silva, Kirk Douglas, Michael Douglas, Tony Curtis, Lauren Bacall, Paul Newman, Dustin Hoffman, Elliott Gould, George Segal, Bette Midler, and

Debra Winger, the star of such hit movies as *Urban Cowboy* (1980), *An Officer and a Gentleman* (1982), and *Terms of Endearment* (1983), is a descendant of Jewish immigrants from Hungary. Winger, born in Cleveland, Ohio, in 1955, identified strongly with her Jewish background and even considered becoming a citizen of Israel. After she graduated from high school, she worked for a while on an Israeli kibbutz (a cooperative community in which all the residents share the results of their labor). After a short period of training with the Israeli army, however, Winger decided to retain her U.S. citizenship.

One of America's most outstanding Jewish-American filmmakers is Woody Allen, a multitalented writer, actor, and director. Allen, whose original name was Allen Stewart Konigsberg, was born in New York City in 1935. He began his entertainment career by writing jokes for other comedians, then first appeared on screen himself in the 1965 film *What's New Pussycat*. Although most of Allen's earliest work was in lighthearted comedy—with such films as *Take the Money and Run* (1969) and *Sleeper* (1973)—his most highly regarded films mix comedy with serious comment. *Annie Hall*, a 1977 film starring Diane Keaton, is an example of Woody Allen's blend of the funny and the sincere. A great success both critically and commercially, *Annie Hall* earned Allen two Academy Awards, one for his screenplay and one for his direction, and took the best-picture Oscar as well. Other successful Woody Allen films include *Manhattan* (1979), *Broadway Danny Rose* (1984), and *Radio Days* (1987).

Jews were also pioneers in the business aspect of the movie industry. In the early days of film, Adolph Zuko formed his own company, Famous Players, and produced some of the earliest multireel feature-length films. As an independent producer, he was given financial backing by Paramount Pictures, and he later became president of Paramount.

Shortly after the four Warner brothers —Jack, Albert, Sam, and Harry—began making silent films in the early 1920s, public interest in movies began to decrease. To win back audiences, Warner Brothers released a new type of movie in 1926—*Don Juan*, a film with a musical sound track. They followed up in 1927 with *The Jazz Singer*, which had little audible dialogue beyond the songs of Al Jolson. In July 1928, another Warner film, *The Lights of New York*, was the first full-dialogue release.

In 1924, the Metro and Goldwyn film companies had combined and were on the verge of bankruptcy when they joined forces with producers Louis B. Mayer and Irving Thalberg. Mayer, who had once been a scrap merchant, became one of Hollywood's most flamboyant tycoons as the head of the Metro-Goldwyn-Mayer (MGM) film company. Thalberg's career was short but brilliant. He had grown up in Brooklyn, and entered the film industry as a young secretary in the New York offices of Universal Pictures. His boss, Carl Laemmle, took him to Hollywood, where he learned production and rose quickly. Sensitive to public taste, Thalberg was a hard-working producer who took part in every aspect of filmmaking. After Thalberg died in 1936 at the age of 37, F. Scott Fitzgerald drew upon Thalberg's personality and career as a model for the title character in the novel *The Last Tycoon*.

Other Jewish-American producers and directors such as David Selznick, Steven Spielberg, and Barry Levinson have been responsible for some of Hollywood's most successful films. Selznick was the producer of one of the most popular motion pictures of all time, *Gone with the Wind* (1939). Spielberg, who began his career in television, directed the modern classics *Jaws* (1975), *Close Encounters of the Third Kind* (1977), *Raiders of the Lost Ark* (1981), and *E.T. the Extraterrestrial* (1982). Levinson (born in Baltimore, Maryland, in 1942) began his show-business career as a writer for the *Carol Burnett Show* on CBS television and won three Emmy Awards for his writing. He later switched to

working in film and worked with another Jewish American, writer-director Mel Brooks. Levinson's greatest accomplishments, however, came after he began directing films on his own. Some of his most successful films were *Diner* (1982), *The Natural* (1984), *Good Morning, Vietnam* (1987), and *Avalon* (1990). His biggest triumph as a director was the film *Rain Man* (1988), which won four Academy Awards.

In another industry concerned with entertainment, William S. Paley became chairperson of the board of the Columbia Broadcasting System (CBS) in 1946 and continued to have a voice in the running of CBS until his death in 1990. Fred Silverman rose through the ranks of several television networks to become president of the National Broadcasting Company (NBC) in 1978. After leaving NBC in 1981, Silverman produced several successful television series, including *Matlock* and *The Father Dowling Mysteries*.

Sports

Young Jews who wanted to make a living with their fists or pitching arms found many opportunities in the early years of the 20th century. Athletic Jews leaned especially toward boxing and baseball, as did other minority groups, because they were two sports that required little money and no social status. Louis "Kid" Kaplan, the featherweight champion from 1925 to 1927, and Benny Leonard, the lightweight champion from 1917 to 1925, were two of the world's best boxers in that or any era. Barney Ross held both the lightweight and welterweight championships in the 1930s. Max Baer won the heavyweight title in 1934 by knocking out Primo Carnera but lost the crown the following year to James J. Braddock. As the economic status of their people improved, most young Jews turned to sports other than boxing. A rare exception is Mike Rossman, billed as the "Jewish Bomber," who won the light heavyweight championship in 1978.

Many Jewish baseball players made the big leagues in the 1920s and 1930s. Perhaps the best was Hank Greenberg of the Detroit Tigers. Greenberg hit 58 home runs in 1938, just two short of Babe Ruth's magic 60. In 1940, Greenberg led the American League with 150 runs batted in, and in 1956, Greenberg became the first Jew to be inducted into baseball's Hall of Fame. A renowned Jewish ballplayer of the 1950s was Al "Flip" Rosen of the Cleveland Indians. Rosen twice led the league in homers and runs batted in.

Sandy Koufax, a left-handed Brooklyn boy, was the most feared pitcher in baseball during the 1960s. In high school, Koufax was a basketball star and won a college basketball scholarship before turning his attention to baseball. Koufax logged some of his best seasons with the Los Angeles Dodgers from 1962 to 1966, when he led the National League with the lowest earned-run average, the standard of excellence for pitchers. He also won the Cy Young Award—which in those days was given to only one pitcher in all of baseball each year—three times. Koufax was voted into the Hall of Fame in 1972. Thirteen years after his retirement, he returned to baseball as a pitching coach for his old team, the Los Angeles Dodgers.

An outstanding name in the history of basketball is Nat Holman. Holman, who grew up on New York's Lower East Side, became coach of the City College of New York team in 1919, at the early age of 23. He held the job for 36 years. While coaching, Holman also played professional basketball with the Original Celtics of New York from 1921 to 1929. He is credited with devising the pivot position, which had a great effect on basketball. One of the legendary teams in pro basketball, the Boston Celtics, was coached from 1950 to 1966 by Arnold "Red" Auerbach. During that time the Celtics won nine National Basketball Association championships.

Among football greats, perhaps the best-known Jewish player is Sid Luckman. He starred at Columbia University before embarking on a 12-year career of professional football with the Chicago Bears. He led the Bears to four National Football League championships (1940, 1941, 1943, 1946) and was named most valuable player in 1943.

One of the most remarkable athletic achievements of modern times belonged to a Jewish-American athlete, swimmer Mark Spitz. During the 1972 Olympic Games in Munich, Germany, Spitz won seven gold medals, setting a record for the greatest number of medals won at a single Olympic festival.

In 1979, the Jewish Hall of Fame was established to honor outstanding Jews in sports. Many of the people mentioned here were elected, including Sandy Koufax, Sid Luckman, Arnold Auerbach, and Mark Spitz.

Jewish Americans have remarkable achievements to their credit. Although there are more Jews in the United States (slightly less than 6 million) than in any other nation including Israel, Jews are only a small minority within the U.S. population as a whole. Constituting only about 2.4 percent of the overall U.S. population, Jews can claim accomplishments far out of proportion to their numbers. In American life and culture, the contributions of the Jews in America have provided great benefits to people of all national and religious backgrounds.

INDEX

ACKNOWLEDGMENTS The photographs in this book are reproduced through the courtesy of: pp. 2, 87, 88, Jewish Historical Society of the Upper Midwest; p. 6, The Library of the Hispanic Society of America, New York; pp. 8, 10, 25, 41, 43, 58, 60, 66, 70 (left), 77 (upper and lower), 78, 80, Independent Picture Service; pp. 13, 30 (left), Library of Congress; p. 15, Jewish Publication Society of America; p. 18, Chicago Historical Society, photo by J. Sherwin Murphy; p. 19, Bibliothèque Nationale, Service Photographie; pp. 20, 57, New York Public Library; p. 26, California Palace of the Legion of Honor, Mildred Anna Williams Collection; p. 29, Levi Strauss & Co.; p. 30 (right), 31 (left and right), *Dictionary of American Portraits*, Dover Publications, Inc.; p. 33, photograph by Jacob A. Riis, the Jacob A. Riis Collection, Museum of the City of New York; p. 36, American Jewish Historical Society; pp. 40, 50, Jewish Daily *Forward*; p. 42, Radio Times Hulton Picture Library; pp. 45, 51, Museum of the City of New York, Byron Collection; p. 46, Amalgamated Clothing Workers of America; p. 47, International Ladies' Garment Workers Union; pp. 52, 59 (left and right), American Jewish Archives, Cincinnati, Ohio; p. 53, Yivo Institute of Jewish Research; p. 61, Israel Office of Information; p. 62, Kapelye; p. 63, National Archives Gift Collection; p. 64, Federal Reserve System; p. 65, Paul Wellstone; p. 68, University of Pittsburgh; p. 69, Rutgers News Service, photo by Francis J. Higgins; p. 70 (right), Edward Teller; p. 73, Mr. & Mrs. James S. Schramin, Burlington, Iowa; p. 74, Israel Zamir; p. 75, Viking Press, Photo by Jeff Lowenthal.

Front cover photograph: Jewish Community Relations Council, Anti-Defamation League of Minnesota and the Dakotas. Back cover photographs: Beverly Sills photo (upper left) courtesy of Christian Steiner; Peter Himmelman (lower left) photo courtesy of Island Records; Albert Einstein photo (right) courtesy of Library of Congress.

The Mercury Club, a group of Jewish athletes organized in 1920 in Minneapolis.

THE *IN AMERICA* SERIES

Lerner Publications Company
241 First Avenue North • Minneapolis, Minnesota 55401